"Wild Churches" and Chronotopic Tensions: On the Space and Time of Interreligious Relations in Modern Indonesia

Daniel Andrew Birchok

In 2015 in the subregency of Gunung Meriah (see Figure 1), part of the regency of Aceh Singkil in the province of Aceh, a group of Muslim villagers burned down an "unauthorized church" (*gereja liar*), that is, a church without proper permits to function as a house of worship.[1] This sparked a series of events that included the fleeing of predominantly Karo Batak Christians from south Aceh into nearby North Sumatra, as well as the subsequent closing by local authorities of a number of other unauthorized

Daniel Andrew Birchok is Assistant Professor of Anthropology at the University of Michigan-Flint. I would like to thank several colleagues who helped me work out some of the themes I address in this article for a 2016 piece in *Inside Indonesia*, including David Kloos, Annemarie Samuels, and Catherine Smith. They, as well as Duncan McCargo in a later conversation, encouraged me to publish a scholarly version of the argument, which evolved into this piece. An anonymous reviewer at *Indonesia* was exceptionally helpful in suggesting key points at which the precision and clarity of the essay needed improvement, as well as in suggesting literature that I had not considered. The article is considerably better because of it. Sarah Grossman and her editorial team were always supportive, timely, and constructive in their work. Of course, all shortcomings in the essay are my own.

[1] The primary meaning of *liar* in the phrase *gereja liar* is "unauthorized" or "illegal." Nonetheless, *liar* can also carry the connotation of "wild" in the sense of being unrestrained, disorderly, or dangerous. In many of the documents that I discuss below, this latter connotation is evoked. To reflect this, I sometimes gloss *gereja liar* as "wild church(es)" instead of the more neutral "unauthorized church(es)."

churches in the area.[2] A month later, halfway across the archipelago in the city of Bitung, North Sulawesi, demonstrations erupted over a proposed new mosque.[3] Some demonstrators dismantled a rudimentary structure on the site where the new mosque was to be built.[4] Like the earlier incidents in Aceh, the ostensible reason for opposition to this house of worship was tied to the question of building permits, which appear to have been caught up in a bureaucratic standoff between supporters and opponents of the new mosque. Both incidents drew national attention among the press, interreligious relations activists, and Islamic and Christian officials from various groups and denominations.

Far from exceptional, such occurrences are relatively common in modern Indonesia. By some counts, they appear to be on the rise, although they are part of longer-standing patterns as well.[5] In some instances, contemporary controversies have roots in older tensions. The burning of the church in Gunung Meriah, for example, grew out of a longer history of controversies about Christian presence in that region. This history, which stretches back to the 1970s, was acknowledged in the aftermath of the events, both by those who carried out the church burning and the local authorities who invoked it to justify closing other unauthorized churches following the violence.[6]

In this article, I turn to archival sources about these earlier controversies in south Aceh as a way of exploring recurring themes that have shaped certain kinds of interreligious

---

[2] "2,500 Flee to North Sumatra after Church Burning in Aceh Singkil," *Jakarta Post*, October 14, 2015, https://www.thejakartapost.com/news/2015/10/14/2500-flee-north-sumatra-after-church-burning-aceh-singkil.html; "Gereja Dibakar di Aceh Singkil, Inilah Dugaan Penyebabnya," *Tempo.co*, October 13, 2015, https://nasional.tempo.co/read/709143/gereja-dibakar-di-aceh-singkil-inilah-dugaan-penyebabnya; "Indonesia's Aceh Province Tears Down Churches after Religious Violence," *Reuters*, October 19, 2015, https://uk.reuters.com/article/uk-indonesia-aceh-violence-idUKKCN0SD0GI20151019; "Kronologi Pembakaran Gereja di Aceh Singkil," *Beritagar.id*, October 14, 2015, https://beritagar.id/artikel/berita/kronologi-pembakaran-gereja-di-singkil-aceh.

[3] "Kasus Masjid Bitung, Warga: Tak Ada Penolakan Semua Damai," *Satu Harapan*, November 13, 2015, http://www.satuharapan.com/read-detail/read/kasus-masjid-bitung-warga-tak-ada-penolakan-semua-damai; "Selama 10 Tahun, Lima Pembangunan Masjid di Bitung Digagalkan," *Republika.co.id*, November 10, 2015, https://www.republika.co.id/berita/dunia-islam/islam-nusantara/15/11/10/nxll1v301-selama-10-tahun-lima-pembangunan-masjid-di-bitung-digagalkan.

[4] "Pembangunan Masjid di Bitung Deserang Sekelompok Warga," *Republika.co.id*, November 10, 2015, https://republika.co.id/berita/nxleq6361/pembangunan-masjid-di-bitung-diserang-sekelompok-warga-part2; "Umat Kristen Serang Pembangunan Masjid, Kota Bitung Mencekam," *Satu Harapan*, November 11, 2015, http://www.satuharapan.com/read-detail/read/umat-kristen-serang-pembangunan-masjid-kota-bitung-mencekam.

[5] The Setara Institute notes a drop in frequency of such incidents between 2010 and 2017, but an uptick in 2018. See Septi Satriani, Yogi Setya Permana, and Ismail Hasani, "Mengatasi Polemik Pendirian Rumah Ibadat," *Policy Brief* 2, no. 1 (2019): 1–2. More generally, there is evidence that such occurrences increased slowly over the course of the New Order regime (1966–98), and then significantly after its end. See Melissa Crouch, "Implementing the Regulation on Places of Worship in Indonesia: New Problems, Local Politics, and Court Action" *Asian Studies Review* 34 (December 2010): 403–19; Desi Purnamasari, "Problem Umat Agama Minoritas: Susah Mendirikan Rumah Ibadah," *Tirto.id*, May 16, 2019, https://tirto.id/problem-umat-agama-minoritas-susah-mendirikan-rumah-ibadah-dJeE. On the New Order foundations of these kinds of controversies, see Jan S. Aritonang, *Sejarah Perjumpaan Kristen dan Islam di Indonesia* (Jakarta: PT BPK Gunung Mulia, 2006), 379–406; Mujiburrahman, *Feeling Threatened: Muslim-Christian Relations in Indonesia's New Order* (Leiden: Amsterdam University Press, 2006), 57–62, 104.

[6] "Gereja Dibakar di Aceh Singkil, Bukan Kasus Pertama," *Tempo.co*, October 13, 2015, https://nasional.tempo.co/read/709149/gereja-dibakar-di-aceh-singkil-bukan-kasus-pertama/full&view=ok; "Kronologi Pembakaran."

tensions in Indonesia.[7] Specifically, I argue that in modern Indonesia particular assumptions about the intersection of religion, space, and time have tended to frame confrontations over minority houses of worship, as well as other instances in which religiously marked people and objects are taken to be threateningly out of place in the archipelago. One of these framings takes Indonesian history as a series of religious conversions, and the other identifies Indonesian territory as discreet units belonging to particular religious and ethnic groups. We might think of these ways of linking Indonesian territory and history as what the semiotician and literary theorist Mikhail Bakhtin called chronotopes, that is, models that conjoin space and time in particular ways, and that underpin narrative types or ways of understanding the world.[8] Of course, a great diversity of factors are always at play in any particular instance of interreligious tension in Indonesia.[9] Nonetheless, the aforementioned chronotopes structure narrative and bureaucratic framings of interreligious conflict in ways that can powerfully amplify their moral resonances, making them recognizable as specific kinds of moral dramas for the parties to them.

I argue that these chronotopes, which I describe in more detail in what follows, and the framings of interreligious relations that they structure and reinforce, participate in what Jeremy Menchik has termed "godly nationalism."[10] Analyzing Indonesia's religiously pluralist, though not liberally secular, political tradition, Menchik argues that the place of religion in Indonesian public life is characterized by relatively shared assumptions about the nature of religion as fundamental to human life and society. These assumptions underpin an Indonesian version of consociationalism, whereby relatively self-governing and nominally independent groups share rights and prerogatives in a system of shared governance.[11] In the Indonesian case, these groups are state-recognized religions, which mediate a citizenship predicated on religious belonging rather than individual rights and protections.[12] The exigencies of governance, combined with godly nationalism's central assumption that proper citizenship is constituted through religious belonging, involves the Indonesian state in both the adjudication of orthodoxy and orthopraxy *within* state-recognized religions and the regulation of tensions *between* them.

While I generally find Menchik's formulation of godly nationalism compelling, one element of it is puzzling. Specifically, he argues that, "Indonesian nationalism is modern,

---

[7] In this article, I use "south Aceh" to refer to the region of Aceh located east and southeast of Bakongan (see Figure 1), and I reserve the capitalized "South Aceh" and "Aceh Singkil" for the regencies of which it has been a part.

[8] M. M. Bakhtin, "Forms of Time and of the Chronotope in the Novel," in *The Dialogic Imagination: Four Essays*, ed. Michael Holquist, trans. Caryl Emerson and Michael Holquist (Austin: University of Texas Press, 1981).

[9] See, for example, the Wahid Institute's yearly reports on freedom of religion and belief (2008–15), located at http://www.wahidinstitute.org/wi-id/laporan-dan-publikasi/laporan-tahunan-kebebasan-beragama-dan -berkeyakinan.html.

[10] Jeremy Menchik, *Islam and Democracy in Indonesia: Tolerance without Liberalism* (Cambridge, UK: Cambridge University Press, 2016), 17, 65–92.

[11] Menchik, *Islam and Democracy*, 133–34, 146.

[12] As of 2021 these state-recognized religions include Islam, Catholicism, Protestantism, Hinduism, Buddhism, and Confucianism; however, a 2017 Constitutional Court ruling has expanded the possibilities of claiming religious affiliations outside of these categories. See Tom Allard and Jessica Damiana, "Indonesian Court Recognizes Native Religions in Landmark Ruling," *Reuters*, November 7, 2017, https://www.reuters.com/article/us-indonesia-religion/ indonesian-court-recognizes-native-religions-in-landmark-ruling-idUSKBN1D71J2.

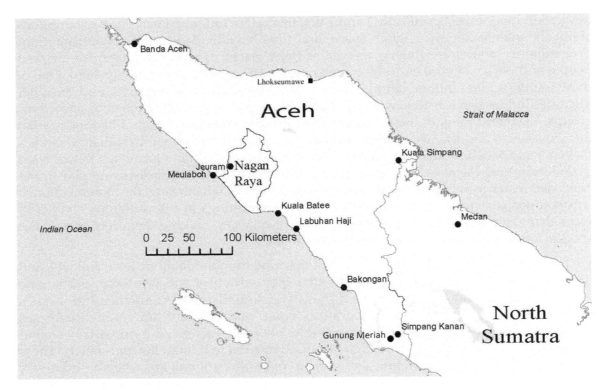

Figure 1: Map of Aceh. Created by Daniel Birchok and Nicole Scholtz
using ArcGIS and open-source databases.

plural, and predicated on theological *rather than geographic* or religious exclusion."[13] Here he clearly intends to emphasize that in modern Indonesia, at least according to the state ideologies that he associates with godly nationalism, exclusions between proper and improper citizens should not be drawn along regional or religious boundaries, but between the religious and the nonreligious. Nonetheless, in carrying out his research, Menchik conducted surveys that asked respondents to comment on the appropriateness of building minority houses of worship in regions dominated by members of a different religion, as well as similar questions regarding, for example, the appropriateness of a regional religious minority holding high political office.[14] These questions were meant to gauge the extent to which his respondents felt that proper interreligious relations should reflect deference to the rights and sensibilities of the religious majority, rather than minority rights and protections. Such an arrangement is an important modus vivendi of interreligious relations under godly nationalism, and Menchik indeed found affirmation of it to be common among his respondents.

---

[13] Menchik, *Islam and Democracy*, 17, emphasis added.

[14] Menchik, *Islam and Democracy*, 148–55, 171–79. Instructively, Menchik used churches in Aceh as one of the examples in his survey instrument, asking respondents whether they agree or not with the following statement: "New Christian churches should be prohibited in Banda Aceh."

This sense that religiously marked persons and objects, including houses of worship, should be restricted in certain regions suggests that the forms of religious belonging structuring godly nationalism are, in fact, tied up in geographic exclusions. I argue that these are not simply the by-product of majority–minority relations framed within a consociationalist balancing of religious groups and their prerogatives, but that godly nationalism is inextricably entwined with common understandings of the space and time of the Indonesian nation. Attending to the space and time of godly nationalism allows one to make sense of how it mediates national belonging by bringing godly nationalism's principles into the experiences and social interactions of Indonesians. In what follows, I illustrate these points by exploring how, during confrontations over unauthorized houses of worship and other forms of interreligious conflict, godly nationalism is called on as a logic of social interaction and moral claims-making, revealing its entanglements with the history and territory of the Indonesian nation.

In making these arguments, I turn to the aforementioned controversies over unauthorized churches that occurred in south Aceh in the 1970s, offering an account of these events that draws primarily from the archival record located in the papers of the Acehnese Islamic Scholars Council (*Majelis Ulama Daerah Istimewa Aceh*).[15] These papers, which are filed in the Acehnese Provincial Archive in Banda Aceh, stretch back to the 1960s, when the Islamic Scholars Council began to closely monitor, and at times intervene in, the controversies over unauthorized churches in south Aceh. The council continued to be involved in these controversies through the 1970s, until the Indonesian national government brokered an end to the tensions, at least for a time. In my analysis of the related documents, I demonstrate how two interrelated chronotopes emerge from the claims that were made by those involved in opposition to churches in the region, including local, provincial, and national figures. The first involves an accounting of histories of religious conversions in the space and time of the archipelago, and comes in two versions in the documents: an explicit narrative of "Christianization" (*kristenisasi*) and an implicit narrative of Islamization. The second construes the Indonesian archipelago to be constituted by regions inhabited by specific kinds of religiously defined people, objects, and characteristics.

Extrapolating these chronotopes from an instance in Aceh, and using them to make arguments about interreligious relations more generally in Indonesia, may seem problematic to some, given the province's reputation for religious fervor and Acehnese nationalist sentiment.[16] However, the parties to the tensions in Aceh in the 1970s were not advocates of an independent Aceh and frequently appealed to Indonesian nationalism. Further, already in the 1960s, related controversies in the regency of West Aceh had informed legislative and bureaucratic debate and

---

[15] Until 1975, when it was incorporated into the branch network of the newly formed Indonesian Islamic Scholars Council (*Majelis Ulama Indonesia*), this council was known as the *Madjelis Ulama Daerah Atjeh* (Region of Aceh Islamic Scholars Council) and then the *Madjelis Permusjawaratan Ulama Propinsi Daerah Istimewa Atjeh* (Special Region of Aceh Islamic Scholars Consultative Council). Although I analyze archival materials from both the pre- and post-1975 eras, for ease of reference, I will refer to the council throughout this article as the Acehnese Islamic Scholars Council. For a history of the council, which in 1999 again became independent and was renamed the *Majelis Permusyawaratan Ulama* (Islamic Scholars Consultative Council), see R. Michael Feener, *Shari'a and Social Engineering: The Implementation of Islamic Law in Contemporary Aceh, Indonesia* (Oxford, UK: Oxford University Press, 2013), 97–128.

[16] Edward Aspinall, *Islam and Nation: Separatist Rebellion in Aceh, Indonesia* (Stanford, CA: Stanford University Press, 2009).

policy-making at the national level.[17] By the 1970s Aceh had become a "laboratory" for New Order experiments with bureaucratic practices of rule that would be applied to the archipelago at large in subsequent years.[18]

Most importantly, the ways in which opponents of Christian churches in south Aceh framed their objections in the 1970s resemble more recent instances involving controversies over houses of worship and other forms of interreligious tension, including those taking place elsewhere in the archipelago. After my analysis of the documents related to the tensions of the 1970s, I turn to some of these later instances in order to illustrate their continuities with the earlier cases in south Aceh. I show how the aforementioned chronotopes continue to inflect legal and bureaucratic frameworks that are meant to address the tensions that underpin such controversies, but that often seem to contribute to them. I do not intend to argue or imply that most Indonesians would find the assumptions embedded in these chronotopes compelling in the abstract, although I suspect many would. Nonetheless, they represent important forms of implicit and commonly shared knowledge that frame controversies of the kind that I consider here. As such, even if one finds them unconvincing in the abstract, the way they link religiously marked persons and objects to specific territories becomes difficult to argue against when they enter public discourse. I close the article by showing how the idea of "archipelago Islam" (*Islam nusantara*), which has been forwarded as a frame for enhancing interreligious cooperation, is itself a reconfiguration of the two chronotopes that have so often informed controversies over minority houses of worship in Indonesia.

A Decade of Tensions in Simpang Kanan

On August 18, 1978, Muhammad Hamzah and Sabarin AS, two men representing a body calling itself the "Islamic Community of the Subregency of Simpang Kanan" (*Ummat Islam Kecamatan Simpang Kanan*), appeared before the Acehnese Islamic Scholars Council. The two made the trek to Aceh's provincial capital of Banda Aceh from their remote home of the subregency of Simpang Kanan (see Figure 1), which was at that time part of the regency of South Aceh. These men made this roughly five-hundred-kilometer journey in order to explain a series of events that led to the burning of four "wild churches" (*gereja liar*), buildings used for Christian worship without the proper permits, in their home subregency.

According to reports that Hamzah and Sabarin brought with them, the church burnings, which occurred in March, were precipitated by a decade of "the growth of the Christian religion" (*perkembangan . . . agama Kristen*) in the region.[19] The reports complained that the provincial government had not acted decisively to address the situation, causing a sense of aggrievement among Simpang Kanan's Muslim residents. This resulted in members of the community finding themselves "unable to

---

[17] Aritonang, *Sejarah Perjumpaan*, 382–405; Mujiburrahman, *Feeling Threatened*, 57–62.

[18] Feener, *Shari'a and Social Engineering*, 2–6, 42–47.

[19] "Pelapuran Utusan Ummat Islam Kecamatan Simpang Kanan Kepada Majelis Ulama Propinsi Daerah Istimewa Aceh tentang Perkembangan/Kegiatan Agama Kristen di Kec. Simpang Kanan Kabupaten Aceh Selatan," August 18, 1978, filed in Arsip Majelis Ulama Indonesia-Daerah Istimewa Aceh (1967–1982), Folder 234, Box 36, Arsip Propinsi, Banda Aceh.

remain patient" (*tidak mampu bersabar lagi*), leading to violent confrontations and the aforementioned attacks on churches.[20] The signatories of a letter of explanation that Hamzah and Sabarin carried with them tasked the men with delivering the report and explaining this state of affairs to the Islamic Scholars Council. It was hoped that this would register the disappointment of Muslims in Simpang Kanan and lead to a remedying of the situation.[21]

One can use the report delivered to the Acehnese Islamic Scholars Council, together with a series of other documents filed with it in the council's archive, to reconstruct these tensions as they were represented from the standpoint of three overlapping and interested parties: local Muslim groups who felt impinged on by Christian migrants, representatives of the Acehnese Islamic Scholars Council, and a network of national-level elites who took interest in the issue of churches in Aceh as part of their formulations of an Islamically informed politics.[22] While each of these parties saw the controversy through slightly different lenses, they agreed on several key points. First and foremost, the tensions revolved around laborers whom the sources identified as "immigrants" (*pendatang*) and who had crossed into the southern regions of Aceh along the province's border with North Sumatra (see Figure 1). Predominantly Christian, both Protestant and Catholic, these groups came to Aceh in order to engage in agricultural work in south Aceh's plantation economy. They desired to build houses of worship once they arrived; however, such buildings required the bureaucratic approval of local authorities, and this proved difficult to achieve.[23] Unable to obtain the permits needed to legally construct churches, they used public buildings not permitted for Christian worship, or they held religious services in private homes.

In the documents carried to Banda Aceh by Hamzah and Sabarin, as well as related papers found in the files of the Acehnese Islamic Scholars Council, these "wild churches" (*gereja liar*) were construed as affronts to local Muslim sensibilities. They were understood to "stand out" (*menonjol*) in ways deemed inappropriate for an establishment of a minority religion, and their critics alleged that they were anchor points for activities—most notably proselytization, but also such things as dressing immodestly, trafficking in pig meat, and selling alcohol—that were found unbecoming of immigrants in an Acehnese "homeland" (*kampung halaman*).[24] Understanding these activities as threatening to Acehnese religious life, both civil society groups and official authorities in south Aceh took action against unauthorized churches, as well as worked to restrict the ability of Christians to found churches legally.

---

[20] "Landasan Pemikiran Umat Islam Kec. Simpang Kanan," June 25, 1978, filed in Arsip Majelis Ulama Indonesia-Daerah Istimewa Aceh (1967–1982), Folder 234, Box 36, Arsip Propinsi, Banda Aceh.

[21] "Surat-Keterangan," July 19, 1978, filed in Arsip Majelis Ulama Indonesia-Daerah Istimewa Aceh (1967–1982), Folder 234, Box 36, Arsip Propinsi, Banda Aceh.

[22] It would be of great interest to consider these incidents from the standpoint of sources produced by Christians involved in the controversies. Such sources, however, do not appear in the archive of the Acehnese Islamic Scholars Council.

[23] On the requirement to obtain approval from local authorities, see Crouch, "Implementing the Regulation," 404–06. Also, see further discussion throughout this article.

[24] Tgk. M. Ali Budiman and Syarbaini Lubis, Letter to Subregency of Simpang Kanan Leadership, April 19, 1975, filed in Arsip Majelis Ulama Indonesia-Daerah Istimewa Aceh (1967–1982), Folder 234, Box 36, Arsip Propinsi, Banda Aceh; "Landasan Pemikiran"; "Pernyataan Ummat Islam Kecamatan Simpang Kanan Singkel Kabupaten Aceh Selatan," September 17, 1979, filed in Arsip Majelis Ulama Indonesia-Daerah Istimewa Aceh (1967–1982), Folder 234, Box 36, Arsip Propinsi, Banda Aceh.

In the decade before the church burnings of March 1978, there were at least three major periods of confrontation related to these dynamics. In the late 1960s, local branches of prominent Islamic organizations, political parties, and labor federations—including Muhammadiyah, Partai Nahdlatul Ulama (NU), Partai Islam Pergerakan Tarbiyah Islamiyah (Perti), and Gabungan Serikat Buruh Islam Indonesia (GASBIINDO)—made calls for the government to more robustly attend to unauthorized Christian churches in the region.[25] They also objected to the promotion of non-Muslims as village and subregency heads.[26] In November 1968 the regency-level legislature of South Aceh issued a decision pushing the government (presumably referring to provincial authorities) to end missionary activities in south Aceh, as well as to not allow the building of unauthorized churches in the region and to not issue permission to found new churches there.[27] This occurred in the midst of national debates over such houses of worship that had been precipitated by a high-profile case of opposition to a church built in the Acehnese city of Meulaboh. Those debates eventually resulted in a 1969 Joint Decree by the Ministers of Religious and Internal Affairs, which emphasized the seeking of local approval for new houses of worship and put the onus on local and provincial authorities to regulate the granting of such approval.[28] This new law, and the debates over the church in Meulaboh that led to it, informed subsequent confrontations over unauthorized churches in south Aceh.

Following this initial period, issues surrounding churches in south Aceh seemed to recede to the background of public life. Then, in 1975, emotions in Simpang Kanan flared again, this time over the building of a Catholic church in the village of Mandumpang. The new building was opposed not only by local Muslim groups, including the subregency-level Islamic Scholars Council, but by representatives of the Batak Protestant Christian Church (Huria Kristen Batak Protesten, HKBP) and practitioners of the indigenous Karo "Pambi religion" (I., *agama Pambi*).[29] Indeed, just as opposition to the new Catholic church began to grow, the Acehnese governor, Muzakir Walad, banned the use of private homes as churches.[30] This not only further restricted the ability of Christians to worship in the province, but also marked a shift in the administrative scale of the controversy, garnering legal action from provincial elites.

Perhaps unsurprisingly, tensions appeared to deepen once hitherto ambiguously legal temporary churches in private homes were formally outlawed, and a third round of much more intense confrontations began in 1977. Governor Walad became involved in a controversy surrounding the establishment of a building for the Indonesian Church of God (Gereja Tuhan Indonesia, GTI), issuing letters clarifying that permission to found such a church had not been granted by the provincial government, nor had its leader

---

[25] "Pelapuran Utusan."

[26] "Pelapuran Utusan."

[27] "Landasan Pemikiran."

[28] Melissa Crouch, "Regulating Places of Worship in Indonesia: Upholding Freedom of Religion for Religious Minorities?," *Singapore Journal of Legal Studies* (July 2007): 96–116, 98; Mujiburrahman, Feeling Threatened, 57–62.

[29] Budiman and Lubis, Letter to Subregency; "Pelapuran Utusan." Note that the reference attesting to opposition by non-Muslim groups is cited in "Pelapuran Utusan," but not dated. I have not been able to locate the original document.

[30] "Landasan Pemikiran." Note that this preceded the parallel national regulation banning the use of private homes as houses of worship, which was issued by the Department of Internal Affairs six months later. Crouch, "Implementing the Regulation," 405.

been granted permission to preach.[31] It was, in fact, four GTI churches that were burned down in March 1978. This was followed by a second round of related violence, including six more church burnings in 1979, a year after Hamzah and Sabarin visited provincial authorities in Banda Aceh.[32] It was only then, when officials from the Indonesian national government stepped in to broker a "customary practice ceremony" (*upacara adat*), that tensions eased.[33]

"Priests and Ministers Illicitly Crossing the Tapanuli–Aceh Border"

The controversies that arose in Simpang Kanan in the 1970s grew out of a deeper history in the region, albeit in ways that sometimes obscured the complexities of the past. In the various documents produced about south Aceh's unauthorized churches, two general features were prominent, aside from the obvious emphasis on the alleged illegality of the churches in question. These included attention to the movement of Christians into Aceh and an emphasis on the provincial border between Aceh and North Sumatra that these migrants crossed. These concerns were most concisely expressed in a line from one of the documents carried by Hamzah and Sabarin, which pleaded with the authorities to "Immediately control the Priests and Ministers who regularly arrive illicitly crossing the Tapanuli–Aceh Border."[34]

While no doubt sounding intuitive to those who authored it, such a statement elided the complex history of the border region in which Simpang Kanan is located. David Kloos draws attention to how in 1840, as the Dutch colonial army pressed inland after taking the port of Singkil, it encountered "a diversity of communities, governed by chiefs of Acehnese, Malay, Nias, Batak, and Mandailing background."[35] This reflected both the region's history of pepper cultivation, which had long spurred migration to the region, and longer-term cycles of political expansion and contraction experienced over the centuries by the precolonial Acehnese sultanate. Thus, in the mid-nineteenth century, when colonial officials began to intervene in the affairs of the people who populated this region, they found an assorted mix of religions and ethnicities.

Kloos argues that the subsequent history of colonial administration of this region involved a process of erasing its cosmopolitan past. Singkil and its hinterlands, having been wrested away from the influence of the still independent Acehnese sultanate, were made part of the region of Tapanuli. The land was only "returned" to Aceh in 1905, over three decades after the Dutch began forcibly annexing Aceh proper to their colony in 1873. Meanwhile, the Dutch encouraged Christian missionary activity in Tapanuli in the hope that a Christianized region bordering Aceh would serve as a "wedge" between

---

[31] "Landasan Pemikiran."

[32] "Berita dan Komentar," *Panji Masyarakat* 281 (October 15, 1979): 10–11; "Berita dan Komentar," *Panji Masyarakat* 282 (November 1, 1979): 10–12; "Dari Hati ke Hati: Kerukunan Hidup Beragama," Panji Masyarakat 281 (October 15, 1979): 6–9; Fauzan, "Menanggapi Pengaduan Pembakaran Gereja di Simpang Kanan Aceh Selatan," *Panji Masyarakat* 281 (October 15, 1979): 8.

[33] "Berita dan Komentar," November 1, 1979.

[34] "Landasan Pemikiran." Tapanuli is the region of North Sumatra just across the border from south Aceh.

[35] David Kloos, "Dis/connection: Violence, Religion, and Geographic Imaginations in Aceh, 1890s-1920s," *Itinerario* 45, no. 3 (2021): forthcoming.

Acehnese Muslims and their co-religionists living elsewhere in the archipelago.[36] Kloos argues that the accumulative effects of such interventions constituted the south coast of Aceh as an isolated region, creating a "geography of ignorance" that obscured its longstanding and intensive precolonial participation in broader and diverse networks.[37] The self-evidence with which Hamzah and Sabarin's report describes the Acehnese–North Sumatran border as dividing two distinct populations reflects such a geography of ignorance.

Indeed, Hamzah and Sabarin's report overlooked not only the region's colonial history, but contestation over the Acehnese border that had occurred in the more recent postcolonial past. At the end of the Indonesian Revolution, Aceh was dissolved into North Sumatra, an event that helped precipitate the formation of the Acehnese branch of the national Darul Islam rebellion, which fought, in Aceh, to refound Indonesia as an Islamic state between 1953 and 1962.[38] During this rebellion, Darul Islam leadership was quick to assert dominion over border regions that previously had not been incorporated into Aceh, in part reflecting dissatisfaction with border-related questions that stretched back to the colonial period.[39] Indeed, for decades after Darul Islam, concern with the Acehnese–North Sumatra border remained a preoccupation of many Acehnese, including the very same Islamic Scholars Council to whom Hamzah and Sabarin petitioned for help in 1978. Throughout the 1960s and 1970s, the council monitored and sponsored activities on both sides of this border, for example, financially supporting recently converted communities of Karo Muslims in North Sumatra.[40] Ironically, this seemed to be an attempt to form a buffer region between Aceh and North Sumatra's Christian populations, reifying the border through a mirror image of the colonial wedge policy.

It is in itself not surprising that a multicultural and multireligious, if contested, region of the archipelago could, over the period of a century, be transformed into a region widely assumed to be properly divided, conceptually if not always in practice,

---

[36] Kloos, "Dis/connection." On the creation of such buffer zones through Christian missionary activity more generally, see Alexandar R. Arifianto, "Explaining the Cause of Muslim–Christian Conflicts in Indonesia: Tracing the Origins of *Kristenisasi* and *Islamisasi*," *Islam and Christian-Muslim Relations* 20, no. 1 (2009): 77.

[37] Kloos, "Dis/connection." On "geographies of ignorance" as a heuristic device in critical geography and area studies, see Willem van Schendel, "Geographies of Knowing, Geographies of Ignorance: Jumping Scale in Southeast Asia," *Environment and Planning D: Society and Space* 20, no. 6 (2002): 647–68.

[38] Nazaruddin Sjamsuddin, *The Republican Revolt: A Study of the Acehnese Rebellion* (Singapore: Institute of Southeast Asian Studies, 1985), 34–82; C. van Dijk, *Rebellion under the Banner of Islam: The Darul Islam in Indonesia*, Verhandelingen van het Koninklik Instituut voor Taal-, Land- en Volkenkunde 94 (The Hague: Martinus Nijhoff, 1981), 284–99. In some regions of Indonesia Darul Islam began as early as 1947 and continued until 1965.

[39] Van Dijk, *Rebellion under the Banner*, 270–86.

[40] Dj. Harun Linga, Letter to Governor of Aceh, Acehnese Islamic Scholars Council, and Muhammad Daud Bereueh, February 22, 1971, filed in Arsip Majelis Ulama Indonesia-Daerah Istimewa Aceh (1967–1982), Folder 251, Box 39, Arsip Propinsi, Banda Aceh; Tgk. H. Abdullah Udjong Rimba, Letter to the Leadership of the Regency of Sidikalang Islamic Scholars Council, April 10, 1971, filed in Arsip Majelis Ulama Indonesia-Daerah Istimewa Aceh (1967–1982), Folder 253, Box 40; Dj. Harun Sinulingga, Abdul Saman Lingga, and Amdjah Setepu, Letter to the Chair of Special Area of Aceh Islamic Scholars Council, January 7, 1971, filed in Arsip Majelis Ulama Indonesia-Daerah Istimewa Aceh (1967–1982), Folder 234, Box 36, Arsip Propinsi, Banda Aceh; "Surat Keterangan Masuk Islam," 1971, filed in Arsip Majelis Ulama Indonesia-Daerah Istimewa Aceh (1967–1982), Folder 251, Box 39, Arsip Propinsi, Banda Aceh; "Surat Keterangan Memeluk Agama Islam," 1978, filed in Arsip Majelis Ulama Indonesia-Daerah Istimewa Aceh (1967–1982), Folder 286, Box 42, Arsip Propinsi, Banda Aceh.

by a border between people of different religions and ethnicities. Lorraine Aragon has illustrated how in Poso, Central Sulawesi, once crisscrossing and entwined religious and ethnic communities came to be socially and territorially segregated as a result of Dutch, and then postcolonial Indonesian, politics and policies.[41] This process contributed to devastating interreligious violence in the region beginning in 1998. Yet this kind of territorialization of religious identity can also frame the religious pluralism of godly nationalism. As already noted, Menchik finds that many Indonesians, worried that the sensibilities of the religious majority might be offended, think it inappropriate for a church to be built in a "Muslim" region like Aceh, or for a Muslim to be mayor of a "Christian" city like Manado.[42] Rather than take this as simply the product of majoritarian senses of group rights, we might instead ask what it means to identify such regions as "Muslim" or "Christian," as well as how such identifications allow interreligious conflicts to scale up to the national level, as they have in south Aceh more than once.[43] Turning to the two chronotopes that emerge from the documents related to the tensions of the 1970s helps address these questions.

"Christianization" and Two Chronotopes of Godly Nationalism

Although obscuring elements of the border region's history, the aforementioned invocation of Christian clergy "illicitly crossing the Tapanuli–Aceh Border" drew on narratives that have long structured the ways in which Indonesians have understood their conjoined religious and national histories. These narratives, in particular iterations of them focused on "Christianization" (kristenisasi), helped make the events surrounding unauthorized churches in south Aceh recognizable as a specific kind of historical occurrence for local, provincial, and national opponents of these churches. They did so, in part, by combining two chronotopes organizing the space and time of the Indonesian nation. The first of these emphasized the successive religious conversion of people and territories within the archipelago.[44] The second constituted a form of what the critical geographer Timothy Cresswell has called "moral geography," that is, the association of specific places, regions, and territories with characteristics and qualities thought proper to them.[45] These two understandings of the space and time of the archipelago have long framed narratives of the Indonesian nation, and the way they informed events

[41] Lorraine Aragon, "Communal Violence in Central Sulawesi: Where People Eat Fish and Fish Eat People," Indonesia 72 (October 2001): 45–79.

[42] Menchik, Islam and Democracy, 148–55.

[43] This phenomenon—whereby local tensions and conflicts come to be recognizable on extralocal levels, sometimes through the simplification of complex circumstances on the ground—has regularly recurred in the history of intercommunal tensions in Indonesia. See, for example, Lorrain Aragon, "Mass Media Fragmentation and Narratives of Violent Action in Sulawesi's Poso Conflict," Indonesia 79 (April 2005): 1–55; Nils Bubandt, "Malukan Apocalypse: Themes in the Dynamics of Violence in Eastern Indonesia," in Violence in Indonesia, ed. Ingrid Wessel and Georgia Wimhöfer (Hamburg: Abera-Verl., 2001).

[44] On this chronotope and its significance in historical contexts not directly under consideration here, see Daniel Andrew Birchok, "Putting Habib Abdurrahim in His Place: Genealogy, Scale, and Islamization in Seunagan, Indonesia," Comparative Studies in Society and History 57, no. 1 (2015): 497–527; John R. Bowen, "Narrative Form and Political Incorporation: Changing Uses of History in Aceh, Indonesia," Comparative Studies in Society and History 31, no. 4 (1989): 671–93.

[45] Timothy Cresswell, "Moral Geographies," in Cultural Geography: A Critical Dictionary of Key Ideas, ed. David Sibley, Peter Jackson, David Atkinson, and Neil Washbourne (London: I. B. Tauris & Co. Ltd, 2005).

in south Aceh both reiterated and reoriented one set of such narratives: namely, those surrounding entwined processes of Christianization and Islamization.

Narratives of Christianization describe an alleged pattern of expanding Christian power and presence within Indonesian society, occurring especially through the conversion of Muslims to Christianity and the transformation of Indonesian public life through Christian political and cultural influence. While always contested, and almost certainly never a majority view, these narratives gained prominence in Indonesia in precisely the decade in which the controversies over unauthorized churches were brewing in south Aceh.[46] In this period, prominent Islamic reformers and activists, most notably public intellectuals such as Hamka and Mohammad Natsir, argued that Christianization endangered the nation, taking it as a neocolonial threat that could reverse the destiny of a now independent Indonesia.[47] All of this occurred in a context in which religious freedom and the proper bounds of missionary activity were topics of intense public debate at the national level. In part sparked by an increase in religious conversion to state-recognized religions in the aftermath of the 1965–66 massacre of suspected leftists, public intellectuals and parliamentarians alike debated whether or not the right to proselytize those who were already members of a state-recognized religion was allowed under Indonesia's principles of religious freedom. As these debates were carried out, it became increasingly common for churches built in regions understood to be Muslim to be viewed with suspicion by Muslims who took them as signs of missionary activity directed at Muslim populations.[48]

While most frequently taken up by activists who, like Mohammad Natsir, had been sidelined from mainstream politics following the rise of the New Order in the late 1960s, it is important not to dismiss narratives of Christianization as marginal in Indonesian history and public life.[49] In fact, narratives of Christianization built on ideas grounded in decades of Dutch colonial scholarship and policy related to the religious history of the archipelago. Colonial officials commonly forwarded histories of the Indonesian archipelago that focused on the region's conversion to Islam.[50] These accounts drew on court chronicles and other indigenous sources, but only amplified certain elements of them.[51] They tended to tell a story of incomplete Islamization, inscribing Islam as

---

[46] Mujiburrahman, *Feeling Threatened*, 41–48, 57–104.

[47] Syed Muhd. Khairudin Aljunied, *Hamka and Islam: Cosmopolitan Islam in the Malay World* (Ithaca, NY: Cornell University Press, 2018); Hamka, *Umat Islam Menghadapi Tantangan Kristenisasi dan Sekularisasi* (Bintaro: Pustaka Panjimas, 2003); M. Natsir, *Islam dan Kristen di Indonesia* (Bandung: Penerbit Peladjar, 1969); Mohammad Natsir, "Sekali Lagi Kerukunan Berhidup Antar Agama: Subangsih untuk Prof. Dr. Verkuyl," *Panji Masyarakat* 129 (June 1973): 16–19.

[48] Mujiburrahman, *Feeling Threatened*, 54–62.

[49] On Natsir's political positioning vis-à-vis the regime, see Robert W. Hefner, *Civil Islam: Muslims and Democratization in Indonesia* (Princeton, NJ: Princeton University Press, 2000), 98–110.

[50] Harry J. Benda, "Christiaan Snouck Hurgronje and the Foundation of Dutch Islamic Policy in Indonesia," *Journal of Modern History* 30 (1958): 338–47; G. W. J. Drewes, "New Light on the Coming of Islam to Indonesia?," *Bijdragen tot de Taal-, Land- en Volkenkunde* 124, no. 4 (October 1968): 433–59; Nancy K. Florida, "Writing Traditions in Colonial Java: The Question of Islam," in *Cultures of Scholarship*, ed. S. C. Humphreys (Ann Arbor: University of Michigan Press, 1997); C. Snouck Hurgronje, *The Achehnese*, trans. Arthur Warren Swete O'Sullivan, two volumes (Leyden: Late E. J. Brill, 1906).

[51] Russell Jones, "Ten Conversion Myths from Indonesia," in *Conversion to Islam*, ed. Nehemiah Levtzion (New York: Homes & Meier, 1979); Anthony Reid, *Southeast Asia in the Early Modern Era: Trade, Power, and Belief* (Ithaca, NY: Cornell University Press, 1993), 154–57.

a relatively recent, and not very influential, addition to Indonesia's social, political, and religious life. This led an influential group of Islamic and nationalist scholars and activists, most notably Hamka, to rewrite Dutch narratives, acts that these authors understood as a form of anticolonial struggle. In their revised versions, these nationalist authors reversed the resonances of Dutch colonial accounts, asserting Islam's deep roots in the archipelago. They frequently took Islamization as the destiny of the nation and projected Indonesia's national awakening onto the archipelago's Islamic past.[52]

While these anticolonial narratives resisted important elements of their Dutch colonial predecessors, both versions shared a basic narrative structure, inscribing the history of the archipelago as the progressive expansion of Islam through the successive conversion of people and territory. These narratives were thus framed directly by the first of the aforementioned chronotopes, that of successive religious conversions: that is, they were histories of the nation written as histories of its progressive conversion to Islam over time.[53] These were moral arguments, and not simply descriptive histories, about who the inhabitants of the Indonesian archipelago were, emphasizing in particular the depth of Islam's significance. In both their Dutch and Indonesian iterations, they tended to imply, if not assert, that the archipelago's history of conversion had established different kinds of societies, depending on when and for how long different regions of the archipelago had become Muslim. Most famously identified with the "reception theory" of the Dutch scholar-official Christiaan Snouck Hurgronje, it was this concern that represented the stakes of these narrative projects for their nationalist authors.[54]

Herein lies the second of the aforementioned chronotopes, a moral geography of people, societies, and qualities thought to properly belong within particular regions, often as a result of the processes of conversion framed by the first chronotope. In fact, this linking of conversion and moral geography was so rhetorically effective that others jumped into the narrative fray as well. The Indonesian Communist Party leader D. N. Aidit, for example, wrote of waves of religious conversions in economic materialist terms, while others emphasized the Hindu–Buddhist past.[55] Regardless of the competing valences of different versions of these narratives, the transformations wrought by the successive conversions described in them tended to be construed in terms that emphasized region and territory as much as, if not more than, people and society. Common narratives of Indonesia's Islamization articulated the idea that Islam had first "entered" (masuk) Aceh before moving through the rest of the archipelago. This identified the territory of Aceh, rather than its people per se, with a uniquely Islamic history and character.[56] Indeed, the moral geographies of the second chronotope depended on such an ambiguity, as the slippage between conversion of people and conversion of regions

---

[52] Bowen, "Narrative Form"; Hamka, "Aceh Serambi Mekkah," in *Sejarah Masuk dan Berkembangnya Islam di Indonesia*, ed. A. Hasymy (Medan: Alma'arif, 1989); Ali Hasymy, ed., *Sejarah Masuk dan Berkembangnya Islam di Indonesia* (Medan: Alma'arif, 1989); Mujiburrahman, Feeling Threatened, 43.

[53] Bowen, "Narrative Form."

[54] Benda, "Christiaan Snouck Hurgronje"; John R. Bowen, *Islam, Law and Equality in Indonesia: An Anthropology of Public Reasoning* (Cambridge, UK: Cambridge University Press, 2003), 46–52.

[55] D. N. Aidit, *Masjarakat Indonesia dan Revolusi Indonesia (Soal2 Pokok Revolusi Indonesia)* (Djakarta: Jajasan "Pembaruan," 1965), 16–32; M. C. Ricklefs, *Islamisation and Its Opponents in Java: A Political, Social, Cultural and Religious History, c. 1930 to the Present* (Honolulu: University of Hawai'i Press, 2012), 18.

[56] Hasymy, *Sejarah Masuk.*

established conceptual maps divided into territories where specific kinds of people, objects, and qualities could be found and on which this chronotope rested.

In important respects, the rise in prominence of the idea of Christianization in the 1970s was simply the latest wrinkle in this process of narrative contestation over the meaning of Indonesia's religious history. It, too, was a narrative of successive conversions thought to have consequences for the character and characteristics of particular regions of the archipelago, as well as the nation as a whole; however, its proponents forwarded it not to make an argument about what the nation was, but to warn against what they perceived as a neocolonial threat to its character. Christianization, as they saw it, threatened to reverse a national unity that was rooted in the archipelago's conjoined nationalist and Islamic awakening. The invocation of Christianization by those who opposed south Aceh's unauthorized churches in the 1970s, including actors operating at local, provincial, and national scales, made this abundantly clear.

The documents carried by Hamzah and Sabarin identified ministers and priests residing in south Aceh as agents of Christianization, suggesting that they had come "from outside the area" (*dari luar daerah*) and even "from overseas" (*dari luar negeri*).[57] Other sources make it clear that provincial officials, including the Acehnese Islamic Scholars Council, saw the tensions in south Aceh in these terms. Already in 1975, even before Hamzah and Sabarin brought their complaints to Banda Aceh, the council had taken steps to develop a programming plan, titled "Overcoming the Problem of Christianization in the Subregency of Simpang Kanan, South Aceh."[58] In it, they proposed "faith immunizations" (I., *immunisasi akidah*) that consisted of precirculated sermons and other religious literature, which were to be sent to Islamic officials in south Aceh to counteract Christian missions there. In the longer term, the council intended to send religious teachers as well.[59] Extending the medical idiom invoked through the idea of a faith immunization, the plan referred to Christianization in Aceh as an "abscess that although . . . treated with medicine . . . sometimes swells until it can be felt painful and bothersome," evoking a sense of bodily invasion constitutive of the idea of Christianization more broadly.[60]

Not only was a concern with Christianization explicit in the documents related to these controversies, but this concern also often brought into relief how Christianization threatened to reverse Islamization, a contrast that depended on the ways both narratives were structured by the idea of a moral geography constituted by histories of successive conversions. The most local sources reporting on the controversies tended to identify

---

[57] "Landasan Pemikiran"; "Pelapuran Utusan"; "Pernyataan Ummat."

[58] Teungku H. Abdullah Ujong Rimba, Letter and Attached Documents to Governor of Aceh, July 1975, filed in Arsip Majelis Ulama Indonesia-Daerah Istimewa Aceh (1967–1982), Folder 234, Box 36, Arsip Propinsi, Banda Aceh.

[59] Three decades later, the province's newly formed Office of Islamic Syariat (*Dinas Syariat Islam*) implemented similar programs directed at the same region, involving the training of "frontier preachers" (*da'i perbatasan*) and "frontier Islamic boarding schools" (*dayah perbatasan*). See Moch Nur Ichwan, "Faith, Ethnicity, and Illiberal Citizenship: Authority, Identity, and Religious 'Others' in Aceh's Border Areas," *Contending Modernities*, February 27, 2017, https://contendingmodernities.nd.edu/field-notes/faith-ethnicity-illiberal-citizenship-authority-identity-religious-others-acehs-border-areas/.

[60] Rimba, Letter and Attached Documents. Interestingly, Hamka, who helped shape narratives of Christianization and Aceh's place in histories of Islamization, was also prone to using such medicalized idioms. See Aljunied, *Hamka and Islam*, 15, 42, 64.

Christianization as a threat to a uniquely Islamic character that Aceh held due to its place in processes of Islamization. For example, the group that Hamzah and Sabarin represented insisted that the 1978 church burning be viewed in light of "historical background" that included Aceh's status as "MECCA'S VERANDAH since centuries past."[61] This common toponym for Aceh indexed the region's history as the first place in the archipelago to have converted to Islam and as the site of several prominent early Islamic polities. Later, the same report identified south Aceh as the birthplace of "Shyekh Abdurauf Syiak Kuala," the last of Aceh's prominent sixteenth- and seventeenth-century religious scholars and an important figure in stories linking Aceh's early Islamic history to the Islamization of the rest of the archipelago.[62] By invoking a second toponym, that of the "AREA OF CAPITAL," the document also emphasized Aceh's place in the winning of Indonesian independence.[63] This title referenced the role that the Acehnese population played in financing the Indonesian Revolution, thereby emphasizing that the history of Islamization cited elsewhere in the document was tied directly to the destiny of the nation.

These toponyms referenced Acehnese territory, identifying it with a uniquely Islamic character that marked Christian churches and other prominent signs of Christian presence in the province as anomalies that ran against the grain of Islamization. Members of the subregency branch of Aceh's Islamic Scholars Council in Simpang Kanan expressed the point in the following manner: "[I]n the midst of Islam has been founded a church, while Aceh itself is entirely made up of the Islamic community, and is a place where the substance of Islamic law is put into practice."[64] Other sources highlighted highly symbolic violations of Islamic social norms carried out by non-Muslims, for example, the passing through Muslim villages by Karo laborers carrying pig meat.[65] Such details established Aceh as a place in which Islam, Islamic practice, and Muslims properly belonged, and where the houses of worship and practices of non-Muslims should be circumscribed. At the very least, such buildings and practices were not to "stand out" (*menonjol*) or be "showy" (*demonstratif*).[66] When they did, Muslims in south Aceh often felt justified in confronting them, sometimes violently.

In interpreting Christian presence in south Aceh as an instance of Christianization threatening Aceh's Islamic history and character, opponents of south Aceh's unauthorized churches weaved a potent narrative. Aceh had become inscribed in narratives of Islamization as the font of Islam for the rest of the archipelago, an idea reflected in the title of one collection of essays about this process, "From Here It Spread."[67] These narratives were very often developed through partnerships between Acehnese provincial and Indonesian national elites with aligned interests in developing and circulating a history of the Indonesian nation rooted in Islamization.[68] Christianization in Aceh therefore

---

[61] "Landasan Pemikiran," capitalization as in original.

[62] "Landasan Pemikiran."

[63] "Landasan Pemikiran."

[64] Budiman and Lubis, Letter to Subregency.

[65] "Landasan Pemikiran"; "Pernyataan Ummat."

[66] Budiman and Lubis, Letter to Subregency; "Landasan Pemikiran."

[67] Bowen, "Narrative Form"; Hamka, "Aceh Serambi Mekkah"; Panitia Penyelenggara Musabaqah Tilawatil Qur'an, *Dari Sini Ia Bersemi* (Banda Aceh: Panitia Penyelenggara Musabaqah Tilawatil Qur'an, 1981).

[68] Bowen, "Narrative Form"; Hasymy, *Sejarah Masuk*.

posed a unique kind of threat for those who found narratives of Islamization to be compelling accounts of the national past. For them, the possibility of Christianization in Aceh threatened to undo at its geographical origins the process whereby the archipelago had gained its unity and coherence as a nation.

Keeping this in mind helps make sense of why and how the controversies in Aceh came to garner the attention of national elites. The 1978 and 1979 violence over unauthorized churches was covered in the national Islamic periodical *Panji Masyarakat*, a semimonthly journal targeting a moderately reformist Islamic readership that was likely to find nationalist narratives of Indonesia's Islamic past compelling.[69] The journal was closely associated with Hamka, who played roles in developing and popularizing both narratives of Islamization and Christianization. Part of the interest by journalists at *Panji Masyarakat* in Aceh's unauthorized churches undoubtedly derived from the ways in which Aceh's place in histories of Islamization allowed controversies over the building of churches in the province to be a particularly powerful illustration of the threat they perceived Christianization to be. While this was frequently left implicit, *Panji Masyarakat*'s coverage took up the chronotopic structure of successive conversions and religiously inflected moral geographies in ways that seemed aimed at making the tensions in south Aceh recognizable to readers who shared this concern with Christianization.

Consider, for example, the following description of how Christian migrants to south Aceh failed to adequately respect the "specialness" (*keistimewaanya*) of Aceh and its population:

> [T]hese new immigrants, who have a different religion and customary practice, have not been able to adapt themselves to the population in the area. . . . Wherever these new immigrants live, they care for or raise pigs . . . [offending] the feelings and peace of mind of the population. Aside from this they found churches at an increasing rate. . . . Contributions for building these unauthorized churches continue to flow from North Sumatra. . . . Did not the Christian community [elsewhere in Aceh] . . . intend to found churches . . . ? But they were attentive to the society around them and the regulations of the government of the Special Area of Aceh in relation to its specialness (*keistimewaannya*). . . .[70]

While elsewhere this article is sympathetic to the plight of Christians forced to flee the violence, this quotation lays the blame for these tensions squarely at the feet of Christian migrants who had allegedly not deferred to Muslim sensibilities or the law governing the building of churches in Aceh. In particular, it takes Christians to task for flaunting the most visible signs indexing their Christian identity: pigs and churches. These objects appear as matter out of place in Aceh. Further, in an article otherwise articulated in the idiom of intercommunal relations, the reference to Aceh's status as a "Special Area" (*Daerah Istimewa*) recasts social boundaries as geographic ones. Status as a Special Area had been granted to Aceh in 1959, along with special rights of self-governance in the fields of religion, education, and customary practice. It was in part an effort by the provincial and national governments to regain the loyalty of guerilla fighters who had

---

[69] "Berita dan Komentar," October 15, 1979; "Berita dan Komentar," November 1, 1979; "Dari Hati ke Hati"; Fauzan, "Menanggapi Pengaduan."

[70] Fauzan, "Menanggapi Pengaduan."

joined the Darul Islam rebellion; but its intellectual foundations were found in the very territorialized narratives of Indonesia's Islamization and national awakening that would already be invoked by local and provincial opponents to south Aceh's churches.[71]

A second article made much more explicit the ways in which interreligious tensions, both the violence in Aceh and interreligious dynamics more generally, were tied to territorialized histories of conversion and its effects. This article provocatively likened Christian presence in south Aceh to "colonization" (*penjajahan*), comparing it to an alleged earlier instance:

> This is what has happened since Indonesia became independent. Muslims have been sufficiently tolerant, for the sake of the Unity of the People, for the sake of the national Pancasila. But beginning with the 1945 Revolution, the lands of the Kingdom of Serdang [i.e., the area around the North Sumatran capital of Medan] have been colonized by our brothers from the Batak lands, aggressive followers of Christianity. . . . [There] has arisen a question: "Is this really the meaning of religious harmony?" [Namely], that the followers of another religion freely let their pigs roam, the founding of churches cannot be slowed down, while the founding of mosques in one's own land and one's own village is difficult? Today churches are founded all the time, and there are also many pigs. . . . Now it is heard that this same method has been used as well in . . . Simpang Kanan.[72]

Note how in this quotation the same morally charged markers of religious identity as in the previous article, churches and pigs, are invoked to index the problematic presence of Christians in a Muslim space. Much clearer in this quotation, however, is the way in which this process is framed by a narrative of Christianization. The reader sees a formerly Muslim region (i.e., the Kingdom of Serdang) full of Christian people, churches, and practices. This Christian presence is portrayed as rather jarring given the history of Serdang as a properly Islamic space. Indeed, the article identifies this presence as a form of colonization precipitated by the movement of Batak Christians into an Islamic region. In fact, it is unlikely that the religious demographics of Serdang reflected anything close to a takeover of the region by a majority Christian population.[73] Here the ambiguity between conversion of people and conversion of territory is particularly productive, as what seems to be at stake is an ostentatious Christian presence in the territory rather than proselytization or changes to the demographic majority per se. Further, in drawing a parallel to south Aceh, as well as noting that this is a story of "what has happened since Indonesia became independent," the author suggests this is not an isolated event, but one in a series of conversions of formerly Islamic territories.

In all of this, one repeatedly sees key elements of the aforementioned chronotopes: successive religious conversions; a productive slippage between whether these were conversions of people, societies, or territories; an understanding that this process resulted in the development of particular characteristics proper to the archipelago and its regions;

---

[71] Bowen, "Narrative Form."

[72] "Dari Hati," 7–9.

[73] Today the regency of Deli Serdang is nearly 80 percent Muslim. See Deasy Simandjuntak, "Jokowi's Defeat in Sumatra and the Future of Religiously Charged Binary Politics," *Perspective: Researchers at ISEAS – Yusof Ishak Institute Analyse Current Events* 79 (2019): 5, https://www.iseas.edu.sg/wp-content/uploads/pdfs/ISEAS_Perspective_2019_70.pdf.

attention to the people, objects, and practices within these spaces; and a concern that new waves of conversion might undo earlier ones. This suggests how thoroughly entwined the chronotopes of successive conversion and the archipelago's moral geography were with the controversies over Aceh's unauthorized churches. Their recurrent reappearance at local, provincial, and national levels suggests they provided a moral language and framing that was recognizable to Indonesians outside of Aceh, thereby allowing the controversies to scale up to the national level.

Finally, the article asks a central rhetorical question: "Is this really the meaning of religious harmony?" This question derives directly from the repertoire of godly nationalism. It calls on its readers to acknowledge that proper interreligious relations require deference to a region's dominant religion and its members. Note, however, that in framing the question of what is the dominant religion in regions like Serdang and Simpang Kanan, the quotation weaves a narrative of territories transformed by the movement of religion and religious subjects through them. Serdang was a Muslim territory by virtue of its place in a much earlier string of conversions, and Christians are therefore "aggressive(ly)" out of place there, harbingers of a progressive Christianization that appears to now threaten Simpang Kanan. In examples such as these, "religious harmony" manifests through deference to the moral geographies constituted by histories of conversion, thereby illustrating the entwined nature of godly nationalism and the space and time of the archipelago.

Chronotopic Tensions Today

It is striking just how similar the grievances leveled in the 1970s by the opponents of Simpang Kanan's churches were to those raised four decades later by the attackers of the church in nearby Gunung Meriah. Both opponents of unauthorized churches in the 1970s and those who carried out the 2015 attack complained that the churches that were destroyed were illegal, having been opened and operated without proper permits. These complaints were paired with similarly recurring ones regarding the flouting of local religious sensibilities, the holding of unauthorized religious services in private homes or businesses, and alleged proselytization. This was in part because the controversies in the 1970s had remained a touchstone of public memory in south Aceh, and some saw the most recent tensions as simply a resumption of ongoing confrontations.[74] Nonetheless, similar controversies elsewhere in the archipelago regularly involve the same litany of complaints.[75]

What are the assumptions that have made these grievances so common? In this section I argue that the continuing salience of the chronotopic vision of religious difference helps explain the frequency of such complaints. Indeed, assumptions embedded in these two chronotopes continue to inform moral claims made about interreligious relations. Further, these assumptions have become institutionalized in important ways in Indonesian legal

---

[74] "Gereja Dibakar"; "Kronologi Pembakaran."

[75] See, for example, "Komnas HAM Minta Klarifikasi Soal Selebaran Pelarangan Masjid di Jayawijaya," *Republika.co.id*, March 2, 2016, https://nasional.republika.co.id/berita/nasional/umum/o3dkwf330/komnas-ham-minta-klarifikasi-soal-selebaran-pelarangan-masjid-di-jayawijaya; Muslim Abdulloh, "Surat Terbuka untuk Bupati Banyumas Perihal Maraknya Gereja-gereja Liar," *Kiblat*, November 29, 2014, https://www.kiblat.net/2014/11/29/surat-terbuka-untuk-bupati-banyumas-perihal-maraknya-gereja-gereja-liar/.

and political life, as well as in how interreligious conflict, as attention to it scales up to broader publics, tends to be incorporated within popular narratives of interreligious relations. All of this has contributed to an increasing naturalization of the chronotopic vision of a moral geography constituted by histories of conversion, even for those who might otherwise reject some of its implications.

A good place to start an exploration of how these chronotopes continue to inflect interreligious relations in contemporary Indonesia are the nation's laws on the founding of houses of worship. Melissa Crouch offers a helpful analysis of them. She begins by illustrating how the 1969 Joint Decree of the Ministers of Religious and Internal Affairs, which governed the building of houses of worship from 1969 until 2006, was designed under the assumption that "the construction of new religious buildings in areas heavily dominated by another recognized religion was . . . a potential source of social tension and religious conflict."[76] In order to mitigate such tensions, the law required the approval of local authorities, who were to take into consideration factors such as "local conditions," before a permit for a new house of worship could be built.[77] In practice this frequently meant denying permits to religious minorities, and resulted in the kinds of pressures from members of dominant religions that are apparent in the documents that were carried by Hamzah and Sabarin in 1978.[78]

In 2006, the 1969 Joint Decree was overhauled and replaced by a new national regulation. Among other things, the new regulation shifted some of the responsibility for issuing permits to a "Religious Harmony Forum" made up of religious leaders of all local religious communities. It also implemented a rule that legal permits for houses of worship can only be issued once signatures of ninety members of the new congregation, as well as sixty signatures from local community members, are collected and approved by local authorities.[79] Given that the sixty local community signatures are presumably not to overlap with those of congregation members, the building of minority houses of worship usually requires that these signatures be obtained from members of the region's majority religion.

Crouch argues that the assumption that minority houses of worship are naturally sites of religious tension has remained a prominent feature of the new regulation.[80] What I wish to draw attention to here is how this assumption intersects with the two aforementioned chronotopes of the Indonesian nation's religious history. Note how the approval of a permit for a house of worship is dependent on the consent of a territorially defined local population, as lists of signatures of local residents must be collected and then approved by the head of the village-level unit in which the building is to be located.[81] Given that in most cases this entails appealing to a religious majority in a particular region, it can effectively mark certain territories as properly belonging to one religion or another. This is consistent with the consociationalist framework of godly

---

[76] Crouch, "Regulating Places," 98. See also Aritonang, *Sejarah Perjumpaan*, 397–405; Mujiburrahman, *Feeling Threatened*, 57–62.

[77] Crouch, "Regulating Places," 99.

[78] Crouch, "Regulating Places," 99–103.

[79] Crouch, "Regulating Places," 109–11. See also Satriani, Permana, and Hasani, "Mengatasi Polemik," 4–5.

[80] Crouch, "Regulating Places," 109–11.

[81] Crouch, "Regulating Places," 110.

nationalism described by Menchik, and could even be interpreted strictly in terms of a principle of deferring to the majority. Nonetheless, the effect of the policy, among other things, is to territorialize the frame through which interreligious relations over houses of worship are negotiated.

In controversies surrounding houses of worship, one frequently encounters statements such as "Aceh itself is entirely made up of the Islamic community," or "[T]he land of Minahasa (that means a Christian majority)."[82] These are not simply statements of demographic fact, nor even always correct. They are instead morally charged claims about in what kind of region one finds oneself, and therefore what kinds of houses of worship and religious practices should be given prominence there. For example, during fieldwork in Aceh, I frequently hear North Sumatra and its capital Medan referred to as "Christian regions" (*daerah Kristen*), even though both are over 60 percent Muslim.[83] Paired with such assertions are references to practices associated with Christians: the drinking of alcohol, singing in churches, and the raising of pigs. In one instance, a friend with whom I was having an argument about whether new churches should be allowed in Aceh retorted, "If they want to build a church, they have a place for that. Medan!" While this association of North Sumatra with Christianity is clearly tied to the province's large Christian minority (between 30 and 35 percent of the population), my interlocutors rarely mention demographics as such, and instead describe the Christian people, objects, and qualities that they imagine to be present in a Christian region.

These assertions of the religious character of such territorially defined regions are caught up in a moral geography that intersects with, but cannot be reduced to, majority–minority relations. Looking more closely at the dynamics entailed in acquiring a permit for a house of worship further emphasizes this point, in part by revealing how these moral geographies continue to be understood as the product of successive conversions. When controversies over minority houses of worship arise in the archipelago, they are often accompanied by accusations of proselytization.[84] In particular, organized opposition to a minority house of worship frequently portrays the supporters of the new congregation as outsiders who have duped nearby residents in manners that evoke, and sometimes invoke, stereotypes of Christian missionaries.

In 2014, for example, after the St. Stanislaus Kostka Catholic Church received a building permit in the Jakarta suburb of Bekasi, the building committee was sued by a group claiming to represent Muslim residents of the village-level district where the church was to be built. Among the accusations in the lawsuit was that the church committee, in acquiring local signatures, visited people door-to-door and brought them gifts of cash and basic food stuffs, methods associated with clandestine Christian

---

[82] Budiman and Lubis, Letter to Subregency; Azeza Ibrahim, "Masjid Asy-Syuhada di Bitung Telah Lengkapi Syarat IMB, Tapi Izin Sulit Keluar," *Dakta.com*, November 13, 2015, http://dakta.com/news/3336/dakta-promosi.

[83] *Kewarganegaraan, Suku Bangsa, Agama, dan Bahasa Sehari-Hari Penduduk Indonesia: Hasil Sensus Penduduk 2010* (Jakarta: Badan Pusat Statistik); "Sensus Penduduk 2010: Penduduk Menurut Wilayah dan Agama yang Dianut – Kota Medan," *Badan Pusat Statistik*, https://sp2010.bps.go.id/index.php/site/tabel?tid=321&wid=1275000000.

[84] Abdulloh, "Surat Terbuka"; "Komnas HAM."

missions believed to attract converts through the distribution of material benefits.[85] In such instances, one hears the echoes of narratives of Christianization, as the process of acquiring signatures of consent from within a territorially defined area can evoke the specter of religious conversion, emphasizing the relative growth of particular religious groups within bounded regions and requiring members of religious minorities to interact with members of the majority in manners that can appear to involve persuasion.

While the moral geographies associated with these narratives of conversion are not always, or even usually, the initial or only causes of such tensions, they can become powerful interpretive tools, especially as religion comes to be widely understood as the fault line along which these tensions break down. This was apparent in much of the large-scale interreligious violence that arose in parts of the archipelago in the aftermath of the 1998 end of the New Order regime. During these conflicts, maps of territory alleged to be claimed or targeted by members of rival religious groups were sometimes circulated by those who feared becoming victims of interreligious violence.[86] We might place these maps in a longer history, including those invoked by figures such as Mohammad Natsir, who claimed that missionaries, engaged in Christianization, had divided the archipelago among different Christian groups and denominations.[87] Similarly, some participants in the post-1998 violence took up idioms of proselytization, threatening forced conversions of rival regions and populations.[88]

What is of interest about these examples is not that they serve to explain the violence, but that they illustrate how easily it could be interpreted, even perpetrated, through a chronotopic vision entwining religion, conversion, and territory. This helps explain why, for example, these conflicts frequently and quickly came to be identified as religious conflicts, and to be fought in those terms, despite their initial complexities.[89] Further, many Indonesians outside of these regions expressed disapproval of this violence, but nearly all were able to interpret it in terms of chronotopic visions of religious difference. When, for example, a television spot featured two Ambonese boys of different religions yelling to each other from across a burned-out city, national audiences rather easily recognized the moral drama.[90] This was true even though the complex intricacies of the earliest iterations of the violence proved far less legible. The tragedy of two boys unable to act as friends because of their inability to leave their respective religious territories was in many ways akin to the story of Christians "colonizing" Serdang publicized two decades earlier on the pages of *Panji Masyarakat*. While having different moral-political valences, both took territorialized expressions of religious difference and history as an important ground of interreligious tensions and the difficulties in resolving them.

---

[85] "FUI Kota Bekasi Kepung Gereja Katolik St. Stanislaus Kostka," *Siar Batavia News*, March 22, 2014, http://siarbatavianews.com/news/view/1849/fui-kota-bekasi-kepung-gereja-katolik-st-stanislaus-kostka.

[86] Christopher R. Duncan, *Violence and Vengeance: Religious Conflict and Its Aftermath in Eastern Indonesia* (Ithaca, NY: Cornell University Press, 2013), 48, 101.

[87] Natsir, "Sekali Lagi," 17.

[88] John T. Sidel, "The Manifold Meanings of Displacement: Explaining Inter-Religious Violence, 1999–2001," in *Conflict, Violence, and Displacement in Indonesia*, ed. Eva-Lotta E. Hedman (Ithaca, NY: Cornell University Press, 2008), 50.

[89] This is a question that has been considered repeatedly by scholars. See Aragon, "Mass Media"; Bubandt, "Malukan Apocalypse," 232–41; Duncan, *Violence and Vengeance*.

[90] Bubandt, "Malukan Apocalypse," 232–38.

This last example suggests how broadly the chronotopic vision of moral geographies tied to histories of religious conversion circulate within the Indonesian public sphere. While it can be easy to dismiss narratives of Christianization or other rhetorical formulations that offer what seem to be openly intolerant iterations of Indonesia's religious diversity, formulations of godly nationalism—which Menchik identifies as illiberal but not necessarily intolerant—rest on these same ideas. As abrasive as it may sound to some, the aforementioned notion forwarded by my Acehnese friend that Christians do not need to build churches in Aceh because they can do so in Medan, represents one dominant formulation of godly nationalism, emphasizing group prerogatives that entail deference to dominant religious communities within specific territories.

Importantly, Indonesian formulations of religious diversity that come closer to liberalism, or are at least perceived to do so by some, also frequently rely on chronotopic visions tied up in the history of the archipelago's waves of religious conversion and its resultant moral geography. Take for example the notion of *Islam nusantara* (archipelago Islam). First officially formulated in 2015 at the National Congress of Indonesia's largest mass member Islamic organization, Nahdlatul Ulama (NU), *Islam nusantara* articulates a frame for religious tolerance grounded in a history of Islamization.[91] Its proponents, which now include not only NU intellectuals, but also figures such as the former rector of the Syarif Hidayatullah State Islamic University, Azyumardi Azra, as well as Indonesia's president, Joko Widodo, argue that the gradual and relatively peaceful conversion of the Indonesian islands to Islam, over several centuries, has bequeathed modern Indonesia with a variety of Islamic practice that is unique, attuned to cultural variation, and tolerant of different religions and kinds of religious practice.[92] In some ways, the *Islam nusantara* vision mixes elements of Dutch narratives of the archipelago's Islamization with elements from postcolonial revisions of these Dutch narratives. It holds Indonesia's history and culture to be fully Islamic; however, it also emphasizes that less tolerant elements of the broader Islamic heritage never took root in the archipelago's authentic cultural traditions.

Islam nusantara has been critiqued in a number of ways by different parties. It is considered too liberal or not sufficiently Islamic by some, and as a backhanded slap at Arabs and other non-Indonesian Muslims by others.[93] However, what I wish to emphasize here is how it, too, is based on a narrative of progressive conversions and the qualities of the people and territories alleged to have been constituted through this process. It roots a specific kind of religious practice, which it presents as relatively liberal and tolerant, to the territory of the archipelago and its Islamization. While contesting narratives of Islamization and Christianization that have underpinned interreligious tensions in modern Indonesia, the basic chronotopic imagination underpinning the idea of *Islam nusantara* remains one in

---

[91] Alexander R. Arifianto, "Islam Nusantara: NU's Bid to Promote 'Moderate Indonesian Islam,'" *RSIS Commentary* 114 (May 17, 2016), https://www.rsis.edu.sg/wp-content/uploads/2016/05/CO16114.pdf; Syafiq Hasyim, "'Islam Nusantara' and Its Discontents," *RSIS Commentary* 134 (August 8, 2018), https://www.rsis.edu.sg/wp-content/uploads/2018/08/CO18134.pdf.

[92] Azyumardi Azra, "Islam Indonesia Berkelanjutan," *Kompas.com*, August 3, 2015, https://nasional.kompas.com/read/2015/08/03/15000031/Islam.Indonesia.Berkelanjutan?page=all.

[93] Fathoni, "Islam Nusantara Menurut Azyumardi Azra, Profesor Kelahiran Sumbar," *NUOnline*, July 27, 2018, https://www.nu.or.id/post/read/93478/islam-nusantara-menurut-azyumardi-azra-profesor-kelahiran-sumbar; Hasyim, "'Islam Nusantara.'"

which specific kinds of religious people and practices are properly rooted to a territory as a result of progressive religious conversion over time.

Conclusions

I close my analysis with the example of *Islam nusantara* in order to make a point, namely, that the chronotopic imagination that in Indonesia frequently frames such acts as opposition to minority houses of worship, or even larger scale interreligious conflict, is not simply the purview of intolerant actors. The proponents of *Islam nusantara* also ground their understandings of proper interreligious relations in the aforementioned ideas about the space and time of the Indonesian nation. Their concept depends on the notion that particular territories are tied, through a moral geography, to particular kinds of people and practices, and that the people and practices proper to these places are such, at least in part, because of a history of waves of religious conversion in the archipelago. This is not surprising. As I have argued, there is a long history of precedents for such an understanding, and the way modern legal and bureaucratic practices, such as the law on the permitting of houses of worship, are structured by these chronotopes reinforce their seeming naturalness.

Exploring this helps us better understand what Jeremy Menchik has called godly nationalism. Menchik's account represents an advance in scholarly understandings of religion in Indonesian public life. He rejects interpretations that would see Indonesia's founding principles, especially Pancasila, as secular in any simple sense, but he is equally wary of describing Indonesia as a religious state. Instead, Menchik identifies Indonesia's tradition of state–religion relations as a form of consociationalism, one that takes religion as fundamental to good citizenship, but leaves citizens multiple recognized religious groups within which to take up religion as a civic good.[94] Further, godly nationalism emphasizes religious group rights and prerogatives vis-à-vis other groups, rather than individual liberal rights and protections.

My account of the controversy over unauthorized churches in Aceh in the 1970s, and the comparative lens through which I have used it to view later cases, is consistent with Menchik's reading of Indonesia's tradition of "tolerance without liberalism"; however, it draws attention to how this tradition has been entwined with models of national territory and history. This is no small matter. Menchik draws attention to how a large percentage of his survey respondents—drawn from Islamic elites from different parts of the archipelago—found building a church in Aceh inappropriate, presumably due to the Muslim-majority population in the province[95]; however, there is no reason to assume that organizing religious pluralism according to group rights and privileges vis-à-vis other parallel groups would result in such a response. The Ottoman *millet* system, for example, accommodated religious pluralism without territorializing religious identities.[96] Similarly, Dutch consociationalism did not assume that proper geographic places existed

---

[94] Menchik, *Islam and Democracy*, 133–34, 146.

[95] Menchik, *Islam and Democracy*, 30.

[96] Karen Barkey and George Gavrilis, "The Ottoman Millet System: Non-Territorial Autonomy and Its Contemporary Legacy," *Ethnopolitics* 15, no. 1 (2016): 24–42.

for religions recognized by the state, even if historically the Netherlands was practically divided into predominantly Catholic and Protestant regions.[97]

Nonetheless, chronotopic visions of religion permeate narrative, legal, bureaucratic, and many other forms of engagement with religion in Indonesia's public life. Such visions are invoked by those who have carried out violence against fellow citizens on the basis of religious grounds, as well as by those who, like the proponents of *Islam nusantara*, attempt to expand the bounds of religious tolerance within, and perhaps beyond, the frame of tolerance without liberalism. These visions are overdetermined by a wide variety of factors: colonial border policy, the narrative contestation of Indonesia's religious pasts and futures by colonial and postcolonial authors, bureaucratic processes such as acquiring permits for new houses of worship, and others. Perhaps most importantly, they help us understand the ongoing appeal of godly nationalism and associated models of religious (in)tolerance. Compelling political ideas, whether high ideals or well-crafted compromises, rarely achieve much in the way of enthusiastic support unless they can be naturalized in the lives of those whom they govern. The ways that godly nationalism interweaves with well-known narratives of the archipelago's religious history go a long way toward achieving this end. Indeed, the frequency with which many Indonesians have and continue to invoke these chronotopic framings of godly nationalism, as they did in Aceh in the 1970s, suggests just how naturalized these frames have become.

---

[97] Arend Lijphart, "Constitutional Design for Divided Societies," *Journal of Democracy* 15, no. 2 (April 2004): 96–109.

Metamorphoses in an Everlasting Present: Desires, Changes, and the Power of Mini-ization in Taman Mini's Stone Age

Roberto Costa

Taman Mini "Indonesia Indah" (hereafter Taman Mini) is the hybrid park built by President Suharto and his wife Siti Hartinah in the early 1970s. The main goal of this park was to actualize their idea of Indonesia and Indonesian-ness through miniatures, dioramas, attractions, and museums. The Archipelagic Concept (*Wawasan Nusantara*), the Five Pillars of the Nation (*Pancasila*), National Defense (*Ketahanan Nasional*), Modernization and Development (*Pembangunan*), and, in particular, the idea of Unity in Diversity (*Bhinneka Tunggal Ika*) are among the key concepts that framed the semantics of President Suharto's political doctrine, and Taman Mini iconized them at the intersection of a Disneyland-like theme park, a living museum, and an ethnographic

Roberto Costa received a PhD in Anthropology from Macquarie University, Australia, and currently works as a sessional academic at the Department of Anthropology, University of Sydney. An early draft of this essay was presented at the panel "Materializing the past and imagining the future" organized by Maris Boyd Gilette and Carol Ann Kidron at the EASA Biennal Conference in Stockholm in 2018. I am grateful to Chris Ballard, John Barker, Aurora Donzelli, Kalpana Ram, Rupert Stasch, Jaap Timmer, and the anonymous reviewer for their helpful comments and perceptive suggestions. I also thank Sarah Grossman for her valuable support throughout the whole publication process. I owe special thanks to Benny for sharing his memories of Bapak Deki and his enthusiasm about the future. The research was supported by the International Macquarie University Research Excellence Scholarship 2016–2020.

open-air park.[1] Hence, by merging customary traits from selected cultural clusters (one cultural pavilion for each administrative province), Taman Mini was meant to showcase, buttress, and convey the idea of a coherent national identity in space and time.[2]

The case of Taman Mini has been widely discussed in different spheres of anthropological literature. In his pioneering semiotic and historiographical analysis of political communication in Indonesia, Benedict Anderson lists Taman Mini among the "non-utilitarian monuments, i.e., those in which iconography clearly prevails over functionality."[3] By examining the progress of Taman Mini's construction, he presciently traces some of the critical relational axes around which subsequent discussions on the park have revolved. Particularly meaningful are those on the relation between Indonesian political power and visual forms of communication (including monuments) and the political significance of valuing replication over authenticity. Thus, his analysis identifies the ideological principles behind the park's setting, which, he maintains, are directed at continuity rather than change.[4]

Along similar lines, Pemberton made a seminal contribution by examining the park as the material consequence of the "Mini-ization" effect, which he identifies as the process of assimilation of vernacular customary practices into the New Order's cultural and temporal paradigm.[5] Salient traits of this paradigm include the domestication of cultural diversity that produces a stable and ordered cultural landscape, and a historical narrative that elides systematically both Suharto regime's violent historical origin (in the 1965–66 mass killings) and the European colonial past.

Moreover, by focusing on Java, Pemberton pinpoints the typical kind of compulsion in the New Order's regime of reframing the semantic of tradition (*tradisi* and *kebudayaan*) according to the regime's ideology (what he calls "the logic of the *meta-spook*," my emphasis).[6] As he clarifies, this compulsion is not merely a top-down process, namely a process imposed by the state on its people; it is also constituted locally, by people

---

[1] Here I refer to the diverse concepts and ideologies as they have been developed by Suharto.

[2] See Benedict R. O'G. Anderson, "Cartoons and Monuments: The Evolution of Political Communication under the New Order," in *Political Power and Communications in Indonesia*, ed. Lucian W. Pye and Karl Jackson (Berkeley: University of California Press, 1978), 282–381; John Pemberton, *On the Subject of "Java"* (Ithaca: Cornell University Press, 1994); John Pemberton, "Recollections from 'Beautiful Indonesia' (Somewhere Beyond the Postmodern)," *Public Culture* 6, no. 2 (1994): 241–62; Michael Hitchcock, "The Indonesian Cultural Village Museum and Its Forbears," *Journal of Museum Ethnography* 7 (1995): 17–24; Greg Acciaioli, "Pavilions and Posters: Showcasing Diversity and Development in Contemporary Indonesia," *Eikon* 1 (1996): 27–42; Shelly Errington, *The Death of Authentic Primitive Art and Other Tales of Progress* (Berkeley: University of California Press, 1998); Michael Hitchcock, "Tourism, Taman Mini, and National Identity," *Indonesia and the Malay World* 26, no. 75 (1998): 124–35; Edward M. Bruner, *Culture on Tour: Ethnographies of Travel* (Chicago: University of Chicago Press, 2005); Michael Hitchcock, "'We Will Know Our Nation Better': Taman Mini and Nation Building in Indonesia," *Civilisations* 52, no. 2 (2005): 45–56; Abidin Kusno, *Di Balik Pascakolonial: Arsitektur, Ruang Kota dan Budaya Politik di Indonesia* (Surabaya: Airlangga University Press, 2006).

[3] Anderson, "Cartoons and Monuments," 301.

[4] Cf. Benedict R. O'G. Anderson, *Imagined Communities: Reflections on the Origin and Spread of Nationalism* (London, New York: Verso, 2006).

[5] Pemberton, *On the Subject of "Java,"* 12–13.

[6] In his ethnographic inquiry, Pemberton observes that the New Order has distanced Javanese communities from their mystical traditions. Indeed, he notes that their customary ceremonies have been less focused on invoking their tutelary spirits (*spook*) than on celebrating the New Order national ideology grounded in these mystical traditions (*meta-spook*).

themselves, who reinforce this logic by consciously or not, adopting it. The combination of top-down and bottom-up processes is thus what secures the "reproduction of [. . .] the desire for culture" in the nation.[7] This point is a central tenet in the spatiotemporal narrative or, in Bakhtin's words, the "chronotope" of Taman Mini since, as I will show below, it permits the perpetuation of those imaginaries and structures of power that hinder any change.[8]

Undoubtedly, as many scholars have highlighted, Taman Mini has undergone a number of symbolic modifications in the post-Suharto era.[9] Such adjustments include the integration into its display of previously marginalized and persecuted ethnic minorities (such as the Tionghoa).[10] At the same time, the emergence of other provincial Taman Mini-like parks has given the park more regional relevance, and, by losing its aura of a mystical place, as it was characterized during the New Order regime, the park has gradually shifted in nature toward a mere amusement park (*tempat rekreasi*).[11] However, as I discuss elsewhere, visits to Taman Mini continue to some degree to be included in governmental programs and international events.[12] New Indonesian administrative provinces are still eager to be integrated into the park's showcase as an acknowledgment of their official existence.[13] The hierarchical and ethnogeographical arrangements of the park's display have played a role in establishing the uncharted and inherently anarchic virtual space of the Indonesian blogger communities.[14] Last but not least, the Indonesian

[7] Pemberton, *On the Subject of "Java,"* 11.

[8] As theorized by Bakhtin, a chronotope is a narrative spatiotemporal construction in which space and time "are fused into one carefully thought-out, concrete whole." Thus, in such a construction, time, as the fourth dimension of space, becomes visible in space; likewise, space is informed by the fluctuations of "time, plot and history." See Mikhail Mikhaïlovich Bakhtin, "Forms of Time and of the Chronotope in the Novel," in *The Dialogic Imagination: Four Essays* (Austin: University of Texas Press, 1981), 84ff.

[9] Michael Hitchcock and Nick Stanley, "Outdoor Ethnographic Museums, Tourism and Nation Building in Southeast Asia," in *Heritage Tourism in Southeast Asia*, ed. Michael Hitchcock, Victor T. King, and Mike Parnwell (Honolulu: University of Hawai`i Press, 2010), 72–82.

[10] See Ariel Heryanto, "Ethnic Identities and Erasure: Chinese Indonesians in Public Culture," in *Southeast Asian Identities: Culture and the Politics of Representation in Indonesia, Malaysia, Singapore, and Thailand*, ed. Joel S. Kahn (New York: St. Martin's Press, 1998), 95–114; Yumi Kitamura, "Museum as the Representation of Ethnicity: The Construction of Chinese Indonesian Ethnic Identity in Post-Suharto Indonesia," *Kyoto Review of Southeast Asia* 8–9 (2007).

[11] Judith Schlehe and Uike Borman emphasize that visitors do not really intend to learn history when they visit Taman Mini, but instead expect to enjoy the facilities and the park. See Judith Schlehe and Michiko Uike-Bormann, "Staging the Past in Cultural Theme Parks: Representations of Self and Other in Asia and Europe," in *Staging the Past*, ed. Judith Schlehe, Michiko Uike-Bormann, Carolyn Oesterle, and Wolfgang Hochbruck (Bielefeld: Transcript, 2010), 57–91.

[12] Roberto Costa, "Harmony Is Beautiful: A Reappraisal of the Aestheticisation of Politics in 'Beautiful Indonesia' Miniature Park," *The Asia Pacific Journal of Anthropology* 21, no. 4 (2020): 352–70.

[13] I refer here to the case of the youngest Indonesian province, Kalimantan Utara (Kaltara). This province was established in 2012 and since then it has requested to have its own pavilion separated from the one of East Kalimantan. However, the request is still on hold since there is not enough land to accommodate the new pavilion. According to newspaper articles, it seems that its construction is perceived to be an important national and political acknowledgment of the new province. See Miechell Koagouw, "Anjungan Kaltara Di Taman Mini Indonesia Indah (TMII)," *Mengawal Kedaulatan Bangsa*, 2016; Farrah Audina, Nur Indah, "1 Anjungan Masih Fase Pemilihan Lahan, 34 Miniatur Rumah Adat Di Indonesia Akan Hadir Di TMII," *TribunJakarta*, 2020.

[14] Endah Triastuti and Inaya Rakhmani, "Cyber Taman Mini Indonesia Indah: Ethnicity and Imagi-Nation in Blogging Culture," *Internetworking Indonesia Journal* 3, no. 2 (2011): 5–13.

government has in recent times attempted to include the park in the UNESCO heritage list for its cultural and historical significance.[15]

All these facts, along with its steady popularity, seem to illustrate that the park maintains some political relevance in the post-Suharto era despite its problematic association with the Suharto regime.[16] Hence, this article attempts to explore the lines of continuity in the park between these two epochs by raising the following questions: Is the New Order's cultural discourse and its compulsion for culture still extant in Taman Mini despite the recent changes in the park? How do reformative projects aimed at authenticity articulate with consolidated hierarchies and structural inequalities?

To answer these interrelated questions, I first reconsider Taman Mini's temporal paradigm by recalling parallels with the parks that inspired it, in particular, Disneyland. I foreground the deep historical and political ties between Disneyland and Taman Mini, analyzing how Taman Mini's chronotope was molded from Disneyland's spatiotemporal setting and imaginary. This preliminary exploration lays the groundwork for a more concrete level of analysis of the park, which is focused on a specific pavilion, the Papua Pavilion.

This specific pavilion is significant because the province of Papua is Indonesia's most peripheral and least developed province, and its historical course of integration into the Indonesian nation-building process has been notably problematic and violent.[17] Moreover, this is also the province in which the fall of Suharto's regime and a series of subsequent ad hoc policies (e.g., special autonomy) have considerably impacted the life of its people.

By adopting a diachronic analytical approach and by giving voice to individuals working on the site, in the second part of the article, I consider how recent changes in the pavilion are reflective of this new political climate. I then narrow down my analysis to a project that is regarded as particularly empowering for the Papuan ethnic group of the Asmat, but which draws on the same logic of cultural homogenization and reductionism that plagues the foundational conceptualization of the park.

My analysis begins with a brief account of the genesis of Taman Mini's project alluding to other official—and unacknowledged—models of reference. This introductory exploration is crucial to elucidate the genealogy of the park and historically situate its ideological bases.

---

[15] I thank Greg Acciaioli for sharing this information.

[16] Despite a sudden drop the day after Soeharto's fall (from seven million to four million), the number of visitors has stabilized to around five million in recent years, peaking exceptionally at nearly eight million in 2012, which was the year of my first visit. Badan Pusat Statistik (hereafter BPS), "Jumlah Kunjungan Wisatawan ke Objek Wisata Unggulan Menurut Lokasi Pariwisata di Provinsi DKI Jakarta, 2007–2013," https://jakarta.bps.go.id/statictable/2015/04/20/67/jumlah-kunjungan-%20wisatawan-ke-objek-wisata -unggulan-menurut-lokasi-pariwisata-di-provinsi-dki-jakarta.html (last updated April 20, 2015); BPS, "Jumlah Kunjungan Wisatawan ke Obyek Wisata Unggulan Menurut Lokasi 2011–2015," https://jakarta .bps.go.id/statictable/2017/01/30/158/jumlah-kunjungan-wisatawan-ke-obyek-wisata-unggulan-menurut -lokasi-2011-2015.html (last updated January 30, 2017).

[17] I am referring here to the controversial annexation of West Papua to the Indonesian state by virtue of the Act of Free Choice, but also the systematic marginalization, discrimination, and violent repression that Papuans have experienced, in particular, during Suharto's regime. See, for example, Richard Chauvel and Ikrar Nusa Bhakti, *The Papua Conflict: Jakarta's Perceptions and Policies Policy Studies* (Washington: East-West Center Washington, 2004).

Taman Mini's Antecedent Models

According to the official historiography of the park, the main models for the Taman Mini project were two Southeast Asian parks—Thailand in Miniature (Timland) and Nayong Pilipino Cultural Park—and Disneyland.[18] The former two were national open-air parks built under the authoritarian and anti-communist regimes of Thanom Kittikachorn and Ferdinand Marcos in the mid-1960s and early 1970s, respectively.[19] Both parks displayed national living traditions (music and dance exhibitions, and arts and crafts demonstrations), historical heritage, and natural beauty (especially gardens and fauna) in a similar way to the Swedish park Skansen.[20] Yet, despite both parks having national relevance, Nayong Pilipino was seen as a central project in the country's nation-building efforts. Hence, the then-first lady of the Philippines, Imelda Marcos, took part in the opening ceremony of Taman Mini.[21]

The similarity of the political genesis of Nayong Pilipino and Indonesian Taman Mini is not particularly surprising if one considers the two countries' century-long European colonization and their strenuous struggle for independence.[22] In both cases, therefore, such a project of mass communication was seen as a necessary medium to convey their idea of the nation to their citizens and strengthen the recently formed national identity.[23]

Disneyland, in turn, was the prototype of entertainment and a symbol of innovation, entrepreneurial success, and consumerism.[24] Conceived by Walter Elias Disney (1901–66) after a visit to the Tivoli Gardens in Copenhagen, Denmark and Madurodam in Scheveningen, The Netherlands in 1952, the novelty of this park was in its attempt to blend previous models of leisure and entertainment formats, such as carousels or fairs,

[18] In addition to these, Soedarsono adds the Polynesian Cultural Center in Laie, Hawaii (opened in 1963), as one of the parks similar to Taman Mini. However, it is not clear whether the comparison is his own, or whether it actually affected Taman Mini's genesis. See Srihadi Soedarsono, "Mini Indonesia: A Fascinating Tourist Attraction," in *Empat Belas Tahun Taman Mini "Indonesia Indah": Wahana Pembinaan Masyarakat Sadar Wisata*, ed. M. D. Purwono (Jakarta: Taman Mini Indonesia Indah, 1989), 88.

[19] See Edson Roy G. Cabalfin, "Condensing the Country: Identity Politics in the Design of Nayong Pilipino (Philippine Village) and the 1998 Expo Pilipino Theme Parks," *EsPaSyó: Journal of Philippine Architecture Allied Arts* 6 (2014): 30; Penny Van Esterik, *Materializing Thailand* (New York: Berg, 2000), 116–17.

[20] Skansen is an open-air museum park established in Stockholm in 1891. It is considered the prototype of current open-air and edutainment parks.

[21] See Jusuf Wanandi, *Shades of Grey: A Political Memoir of Modern Indonesia, 1965–1998* (Sheffield, UK: Equinox Publishing, 2012), 90; Pemberton, "Recollections from 'Beautiful Indonesia' (Somewhere Beyond the Postmodern)," 243–44; 251.

[22] The proximity of the two countries' leadership in reference to the construction of their national open-air parks was evident in reciprocal state visits when Nayong Pilipino and Taman Mini opened: the Suhartos attended Nayong Pilipino's inauguration in 1971; Imelda Marcos participated in Taman Mini's opening ceremony and planted a banyan tree, a symbol of Javanese royalty and the then-president's party (Golkar), in the orchid garden. Orchids, more specifically the anggrek bulan, are also a national symbol by presidential decree. See Cabalfin, "Condensing the Country," 30; Pemberton, *On the Subject of "Java,"* 153, 160.

[23] Timland park was funded by the state as well, although it was not seen as a foundational project like Nayong Pilipino or Taman Mini. Part of the reason is that Thailand underwent a different historical trajectory compared to Indonesia or the Philippines, being the only country in Southeast Asia—and one of the very few worldwide—to have escaped direct European colonization and was therefore in less dire need of remapping national history without colonial rule and stimulating people's national pride. See Van Esterik, *Materializing Thailand*, 117.

[24] The two models are described as places where the nation's culture is shown and promoted.

in a way that heightened their attractiveness. More importantly, this park epitomizes a potent symbol of America-ness and anti-communist values: since World War II, the Disney studios have been a strong progovernmental instrument of propaganda to fight, through their cartoons, any ideology that would challenge American values. Hence, it is no surprise that Walt Disney felt a deep aversion to communism and communists, and during the communist purges of McCarthyism, he even testified against his own workers who were suspected of having communist sympathies.[25]

While these parks were the official models for the Taman Mini project, the real historical genealogy of the park proves to be far richer. The Taman Mini park was most certainly patterned on Dutch colonial museum models, such as the Bali Museum, established in 1932 and based on the 1914 Dutch colonial exhibition at Semarang.[26] The idea of erecting a national park began to circulate more seriously when an English UNESCO development expert, John Irwin, was charged by the Indonesian Ministry of Education and Culture in 1957 to survey the situation of museums in Indonesia. At the end of his survey, Irwin hinted at building a national open-air museum in Jakarta to showcase the wide cultural, ecological, and architectural variety of Indonesia.[27]

Unearthing these stories does not simply reveal the historical genesis of the park; rather, it is important to penetrate the tropes that characterize this setting. Such tropes include the anticolonial sentiment, which is manifested in the park by omitting any reference to colonial pasts. Likewise, anti-communism is another trope of the national narrative of Taman Mini that is used to circumvent any allusion to the violent Suharto regime's historical origin. This trope is realized not simply by refraining from mentioning any historical reference to communism and its role in the process of Indonesian nation formation (*Kebangkitan Nasional Indonesia*). More cogently, it was displayed through a dedicated museum, the Museum of PKI Betrayal (*Museum Penghianatan PKI*), which used dioramas to showcase the Thirtieth of September Movement's violent coup attempt. This museum lies in *Lubang Buaya*, on the site where the bodies of the murdered officers were hidden by the G30S. Despite being just outside Taman Mini's enclosure, this museum is perceived as an integral part of Taman Mini because it used to be a common practice in Suharto's time to couple a visit to the park with one to *Lubang Buaya*.

---

[25] Louise Krasniewicz, *Walt Disney: A Biography* (Santa Barbara: Greenwood, 2010), 105–07.

[26] Kusno, *Di Balik Pascakolonial*, 76; Yulia Nurliani Lukito, *Exhibiting Modernity and Indonesian Vernacular Architecture: Hybrid Architecture at Pasar Gambir of Batavia, the 1931 Paris International Colonial Exhibition and Taman Mini Indonesia Indah* (Wiesbaden: Springer, 2016).

[27] "Another scheme, to which the Government has already committed itself, is for the creation of a new National Museum at the capital, Jakarta. This will combine features of what in the West is known as the open-air museum with conventional museum planning, taking as its theme the national motto: 'Unity in Diversity.' There will be a 35-acre park, around the periphery of which will be erected the most varied and spectacular examples of traditional Indonesian domestic architecture. Each will be placed in its specific ecological setting and be furnished according to local tradition. This part of the scheme will represent the diversity of Indonesian culture. The unity will be represented by a modern functional building in the center of the park, illustrating the links in Indonesia's cultural development from the Neolithic stage until modern times—beginning with ethnological unity, and then showing the stages in technological advance. Another gallery will illustrate the geological features which unite the land itself." John Irwin, "Museums in Indonesia," *Museum International* 10, no. 4 (1957): 279. See also Amir Moh. Sutaarga, "The Role of Museums in Indonesia: Collecting Documents from the Past and the Present for a Better Future," in *Treasure Hunting? Collectors and Collections of Indonesian Artefacts*, ed. Reimar Schefold and Han F. Vermeulen (Leiden: Universiteit Leiden, 2002), 284.

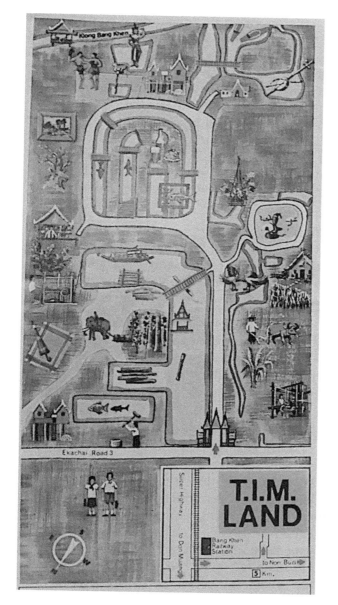

Figure 1. Thailand in Miniature at T.I.M. Land. Map by Interelations Inc. Bangkok, courtesy of Pra Choom Chang, Ltd.

These are some of the founding motives of the park and the New Order's ideology. But how do these ideologies construct the park's chronotope and relate it to the here-and-now? In what follows, I delineate the hyperreal chronotope of the American park and deepen the correlation between Disneyland and, *mutatis mutandis*, Taman Mini.

Spatiotemporal Continuum in Disneyland

As the first plans for the park were being formalized, the Suhartos visited Disneyland in California (May 31, 1970).[28] What pushed Ibu Tien Suharto, the main promoter of

---

[28] See "Suharto Visits Disneyland; Takes Helm of Cruise Boat," *New York Times*, June 1, 1970.

Taman Mini, to "disneytize" the project was the importance of the amusement element, which was seen as essential in sublimating the project's mission (education and culture, *pendidikan dan kebudayaan*) and inculcating in Indonesians the new state philosophy.[29] As officially stated in the publication that commemorates Taman Mini's birth, tradition and innovation in Indonesia (*mendorong pertumbuhan kemajuan teknologi di Tanah Air kita*) are central to the idea of the park.[30] Indeed, the new park needed to display (*peragaan*) the Indonesian archipelago in order to fully depict its potential, appearance, and prospect (*segala potensi, aspek dan prospek*), and communicate the founding features and extent (*pembinaan kepribadian dan pengembangan*) of the nation (*bangsa*). The park thus embodied not merely a model of development, but also, as we shall see, a tool of historical revisionism and political propaganda with a spatiotemporality very similar to that of Disneyland.

Focusing on the spatiotemporality of the two parks, the poststructural lessons by Umberto Eco, Jean Baudrillard, and Louis Marin have taught us that the concept of time is pivotal in the construction of hyperreal parks such as Disneyland.[31] Disneyland, as a miniaturized America, is a park where reality and fantasy—or, better, hyperreality and utopia, respectively—coalesce. The centrality of time has been evident since the opening speech of Disney, on July 17, 1955:

> To all who come to this happy place: welcome. Disneyland is your land. Here age relives fond memories of the past. Here youth may savor the challenge and promise of the future. Disneyland is dedicated to the ideals, the dreams, and the hard facts that have created America, with the hope that it will be a source of joy and inspiration to all the world.[32]

These words, which are now engraved on memorial plaques displayed in Disneyland resorts in the United States, Europe, and Asia, form Disney's manifesto. What emerges is the confluence of past and future that can make everyone happy. Disney's sociopolitical commitment to showing American ideals, dreams, and truths—and proselytizing American-ness against other political orders—is also explicit. It is, therefore, in the negotiation between historical elements and visionary scenarios that Disney carries out his plan of blending facts and fiction—an American hallmark, as per postmodernists— and subsequently subverting the linearity of time and history by making it utopic. This idea is also echoed by another plaque installed over the principal access gate into Disneyland that reads, "Here you leave today, and enter the world of yesterday, tomorrow and fantasy."[33]

The separation from today, or the present, represents a divorce from the real world. This aspect, as Eco argues, creates a higher degree of hyperreality, as the real within

[29] Cf. Suharto, *Sambutan Presiden Pada Upacara Peringatan Hut Ke III Taman Mini "Indonesia Indah" Tanggal 20 April 1978* (Jakarta: Departemen Penerangan RI, 1978).

[30] *Apa Dan Siapa Indonesia Indah* (Jakarta: s.n., 1975), 27, 40.

[31] Umberto Eco, *Travels in Hyperreality* (Boston: Houghton Mifflin Harcourt, 1986), 1–58; Jean Baudrillard, *The Precession of Simulacra* (Los Angeles: Semiotext[e], 1983), 23–26; and Louis Marin, *Utopics: Spatial Play* (Atlantic Highlands; London: Humanities; Macmillan, 1984), 238–57. As a point of interest, during the initial stages of the plan, the park was called Mickey Mouse Park and Disneylandia.

[32] Krasniewicz, *Walt Disney*, 131.

[33] Tison Pugh and Susan Aronstein, *The Disney Middle Ages: A Fairy-Tale and Fantasy Past* (London: Palgrave Macmillan, 2012), 155.

the park's sphere is not disguised (as in a wax museum); rather, it is the visitors' perceptions that are altered. In other words, Disneyland's spatiotemporal blend is the result of illusions and hallucinations (Eco dubs the park a "hallucination machine") that adulterate and distort visitors' understanding of time and reality. The goal is clear: through imitation, fictionality, technology, and illusions, a spatiotemporal continuum is constructed. In this continuum, past and future[34] are no longer differentiated, combined without voids in a spatial arrangement that is "an immense, continuous 'found object.'"[35] The result is therefore a chronotope in which, as maintained by Marc Augé in his supermodern inquiry, both time and space superabound and exceed.[36]

To further understand Disneyland's spatiotemporality, it can be compared to one of Bakhtin's chronotopes, namely the chronotope of the adventure-time of Greek romances.[37] This chronotope is characterized by the motives of "encounter" and "adventure," which both entail abundant space and time. Places and times in this setting are fluid: the blend of real and fiction leaves little room for organic ties between space and time, thus full reversibility and interchangeability of times and places are possible. Moreover, the setting is characterized by the presence of curiosities and rarities that bear no connection to each other and that are as unpredictable as the evolutions of the adventures themselves. For this erratic nature, which nonetheless follows logic and unity, Bakhtin also draws parallels between Greek romances and the chivalric romances, since in the latter's chronotope time is distorted as in dreams.[38] Indeed, in this chronotope dreams are not simply elements of the content, but generators of forms that organize space. This is also one of the foundational principles of Disneyland.

Everlasting Present in Taman Mini

Like Disneyland, the spatiotemporal logic underlying Taman Mini is conceived to celebrate a glorious past and develop a technological future—or ideals, dreams, and hard facts, in the words of Disney. Yet, while Disneyland combines past and future to project visitors into a utopic and dream-like spatiotemporal continuum that excludes the present time ("today," in the words of Disney), Taman Mini puts this continuum in relation to the present time in order to eternalize the here-and-now.

To examine this point and Taman Mini's chronotope, I briefly discuss the element of replication. The relevance of this element is due to its function in the New Order's political communication: as argued by Anderson, replication is indeed "designed to reveal essence and continuity rather than record existence and change."[39] In Taman Mini, as the name of the park suggests, the replicas (usually) take the form of miniatures, which

---

[34] In this regard, Margaret King adds, "No other artform can showcase the interplay of ancient and modern, static and kinetic, tradition and futurism with such mastery and bravura as seen on the unfolding stage set of theme-park history." Margaret J. King, "The American Theme Park: A Curious Amalgam," in *Continuities in Popular Culture: The Present in the Past and the Past in the Present and Future*, ed. Ray B. Browne and Ronald J. Ambrosetti (Bowling Green, OH: Bowling Green State University Popular Press, 1993), 51.

[35] Eco, *Travels in Hyperreality*, 48.

[36] Marc Augé, *Non-Places: Introduction to an Anthropology of Supermodernity* (London: Verso, 2006).

[37] Bakhtin, "Forms of Time and of the Chronotope in the Novel," 86–110.

[38] Bakhtin, "Forms of Time and of the Chronotope in the Novel," 151–58.

[39] Anderson, "Cartoons and Monuments," 311.

should be understood not only as mere reductions of physical size, but also through their semantic complexity.

In this respect, Stewart argues that miniaturizing—or overscaling—physical reality are bold cultural and political acts.[40] It is indeed by altering their physical appearance that historical referents (say, monuments or artifacts) are made accessible and comprehensible (or majestic and mystical when overscaled). Therefore, if one takes the miniature of the temple of Borobudur in Taman Mini as an example, it can be said that its size allows visitors to attend to that reality in a more intelligible, intimate, and private manner. This psychological implication is, after all, the main goal of any miniature park.

However, as Stewart argues further, a diminutive version of a complex reality also has temporal repercussions as it shows "a world clearly limited in space but frozen and thereby both particularized and generalized in time."[41] In other words, the reduction of physical reality produces temporal ambiguity according to which reproductions, such as Taman Mini's Borobudur, are transformed into signposts that are no longer meant to mark the passage of chronological time. Rather, and much more ambiguously, they create a broader and more vague timescape that is atemporal in nature and resonates with the dream-like scape of Disneyland. Taman Mini's Borobudur does not simply refer to the Shailendra kingdom's golden age, but also, and more importantly, to a constructed glorious past that is directly connected to present Indonesia and that brackets the European colonial era.

Another element to understanding how the temporality of Taman Mini tends to eternalize the here-and-now is the hierarchization of space—an aspect that reflects the New Order's centralist paradigm. In this regard, Donzelli advances that Taman Mini's chronotope is characterized by "a vertical spatiality capable of synchronizing diachrony," that is, a hierarchized sociocultural space that flattens history into present time and makes it "frozen in a perennial present."[42] Operatively, this is realized by displaying in specific clusters diverse elements from different traditions through consolidated hierarchies. This fusion is what renders the impression of timelessness or temporal "voracious" present, in that it prioritizes hierarchy over chronological time and swallows up the past and future into an everlasting present.

Consequently, this vertical spatiality capable of synchronizing diachrony equals a perpetual absence of change since "change, any change at all, is detrimental" to stability and order.[43] Even the element of "progress," which was borrowed from Disneyland and is manifested in Taman Mini through the wide array of technological museums (e.g., Information, Telecommunications, and Transportation) and attractions (e.g., 4D motion theatre), is bent here to the here-and-now: these futuristic features are indeed blended with the other material signposts standing for tradition, engendering in this way the

---

[40] Susan Stewart, *On Longing: Narratives of the Miniature, the Gigantic, the Souvenir, the Collection* (Durham and London: Duke University Press, 1993).

[41] Stewart, *On Longing*, 48.

[42] Aurora Donzelli, "Crossover Politics: Spatiotemporal Images of the Nation-State and the Vintage Aesthetics of the Margins in Post-Suharto Political Oratory. Transnational Neoliberal Democracy and the Vintage Aesthetics of the Margins in Post-Suharto Political Oratory," in Tilburg Working Papers in Culture Studies, Special Issue *Margins, Hubs, and Peripheries in a Decentralizing Indonesia* 162 (2016): 82.

[43] Pemberton, "Recollections from 'Beautiful Indonesia' (Somewhere Beyond the Postmodern)," 251.

dizzy impression of absence of time. After all, if, as Michael Wood puts it, Taman Mini was built to become Suhartos' *kraton*, the idea of time and history in the park had to aspire more to eternity than change.[44] In this respect, it can be noted that Taman Mini's temporality resonates with what Lévi-Strauss indicates as "mythological time," that is, the specific temporal pattern typically used in myths, which blends historical and ahistorical facts to render mythological narratives everlasting.[45]

But how has this everlasting present been maintained after the ousting of President Suharto? To answer this question, I continue my analysis by taking into account the Papua Pavilion (*Anjungan Papua*), one of the park's thirty-three provincial pavilions and the easternmost in the Indonesian archipelago.[46] Papua occupies an important place in the Indonesian nation-building process: then-named Irian Jaya (Glorious Irian) was the "trophy" of the Indonesian nationalists during the confrontation with the Netherlands and marked the geopolitical expansion of Indonesia beyond the Malay area. For these same reasons—and for its enormous reserves of natural resources—Papua has been particularly marginalized and its indigenous communities have suffered racial, ethnic, and cultural discrimination, as highlighted by recent protests following the incident of Surabaya in 2019.[47] The paradox of this province is that it is seen at once as a province like any other and simultaneously as the home of a substandard culture beyond redemption. As recently discussed by Rutherford, this paradox is embedded in a history dating back to the Dutch colonial era, in which Papua was "relegated to the lowest rung of the racial ladder" as "a place empty of customary law."[48] Papua is therefore a place in which "atemporality" and "absence of time" are particularly meaningful, and it exemplifies, better than other provinces, the characteristic chronotope of Taman Mini.

The Papua Pavilion and Future Projects

My first visit to the park dates back to 2012. I had just arrived in Indonesia to take part in a program of cultural diplomacy organized by the Indonesian Ministry of Foreign Affairs.[49] The first week of this program took place in Jakarta where we were introduced to the city's cultural highlights. During the sightseeing tour of museums and heritage sites, we spent a day at Taman Mini where we hopped on and off the bus to visit several

[44] A *kraton*, as Wood writes, is not to be understood as the royal palace or the residence of the government, but rather as "a source of otherworldly power, which by representing in symbolic terms the place of the ruler in the cosmos was able to increase that ruler's earthly authority." Michael Wood, *Official History in Modern Indonesia* (Leiden: Brill Academic Publishers, 2005), 25, 22.

[45] Claude Lévi-Strauss, "The Structural Study of Myth," *The Journal of American Folklore* 68, no. 270 (1955): 430.

[46] The construction of the youngest province's pavilion, North Kalimantan, is still under consideration. See footnote 13.

[47] I am referring here to the incident that occurred at the Papuan dormitory in Surabaya on August 17 in which racist abuses by police toward Papuan students were documented in a viral video. This incident ignited a series of other protests across Indonesia that had a vast media echo and powerfully raised the issue of racial discrimination in the country.

[48] Danilyn Rutherford, *Living in the Stone Age: Reflections on the Origins of a Colonial Fantasy* (Chicago and London: University of Chicago Press, 2018), 42.

[49] On the concept of cultural diplomacy in Indonesian foreign policy, see Amelia A. Rezki and Yarang Imron, "Indonesian Art and Culture Scholarship (IACS) for Indonesian Cultural Diplomacy to the International Society: Salad Bowl or Melting Pot," in *Indonesia's Path Toward Middle Powership*, ed. Yohanes Wiliam Santoso, Fitra Shaumi Azzahra, and Emanuella Ninta Toreh (Surabaya: Airlangga University Press, 2019).

Figure 2. Miniature of the Papua Pavilion. (Taman Mini, 2018)

pavilions. Among the several pavilions visited, my attention was caught in particular by the one representing the Papua province, which is located in a quiet spot shielded by thick vegetation, just in front of the Taman Burung (Bird Park).

In my notes, I recorded that the environment of that pavilion was more "savage" and less looked-after compared to the other pavilions I had previously visited. The ethnographic collection, hosted in a replica of a traditional Tobati-Enggros two-story Kariwari building, was dustier and more chaotic. Some showcases were empty, and the dummies donning traditional clothes and accessories were damaged. The semi-darkness of the place and the display of stuffed animals, a mummy, and other "dark" items created an eerie environment. The museum building was surrounded by a pond—which stands for Sentani Lake—wherein a diorama representing eight Asmat men paddling on a traditional dugout canoe was intended to impress visitors with their quaintness. Across the path, on the right, huts reproduced a Dani village (*sili*), but the thatched dome roofs were falling apart. Men's and women's huts (*honai* and *abeai*) were empty inside but for pig cages (*wam-ai*) containing piglet dummies. At the village's entrance, a shield, a spear, and further accessories leaned against the fence: visitors could reenact life as a Papuan for a few thousand rupiahs. Next to the village replica, at the top of a traditional Dani watchtower, a dummy held an Indonesian flag. Between the replica of the Dani village and those of the highest tops of the Jayawijaya mountains (Trikora and Mandala), there was a shed under which a mature dark-skinned man with eye-catching body decorations was seated on the ground in a disheveled lotus position, mumbling while carving an openwork-style miniaturized ancestor pole (*mbis*). A handwritten cardboard sign stood in front of the man, requesting a small donation from tourists who wanted to photograph him.

Figure 3. A replica of a traditional Asmat canoe (*ci*) with "wild" Asmat rowers.
(Papua Pavilion, Taman Mini, 2018)

I concluded in my notes that this pavilion contrasted significantly with the well-maintained and vibrant pavilions of other Indonesian provinces. More than other displays, it conveyed the perceived savageness of this land and its people and the timelessness of its cultures.

Some years later, in 2016, I returned to the park after a reconnaissance trip to Asmat.[50] I did not just want to revisit the park, but to talk to the Asmat woodcarver and to reexperience the sinister and decadent aura I perceived in the Papua Pavilion during my first visit. The park was nearly deserted. I stepped off the *gojek* that brought me there and headed straight to the pavilion. This time the atmosphere seemed somewhat different. The area was far better looked after, and the ethnographic exhibition, which was still located in the Kariwari building, had been renovated: the signs of poor maintenance I previously recorded had almost disappeared. The collection even seemed to have been enriched with additional items, which the employee at the entrance confirmed, and the ambiance was more visitor-friendly. I then decided to visit the woodcarver's shack. The art shop was more or less as I remembered, full of wooden artifacts and souvenirs lined up against the low walls. In the middle, cardboard layers lined the parquet floor; next to them, a hammer, a chisel, shavings, and pieces of unfinished woodcarvings. But the seat was empty this time.

---

[50] The material presented in this section also originates from subsequent visits to the pavilion undertaken between 2017 and 2018.

Figures 4–6. Comparison in time: signs of changes and restoration in the Papua Pavilion.

I asked the lady behind the cluttered souvenir counter about the woodcarver; she told me that he died a few years earlier. He was 86, and his name was Deki Asiam. She added that he was popular in the park, where he had been working for around twenty-four years. He came from the Casuarina Coast (Asmat Southern Coast, Papua) and carved many of the artifacts displayed in the shop. The objects she indicated blended Asmat and non-Asmat (Kamoro) styles and models. She told me, "Asmat and Kamoro arts are very close, like siblings."[51] This stylistic ambiguity was particularly evident around the shop, where authentic Asmat woodcarvings (shields, weapons, bowls, openwork boards, ancestor figures, and drums) were mingled with Asmat hybrids, Papuan items (penis gourds, oars, and hats), and non-Asmat souvenirs caricaturing Asmat peoples' primitiveness (small wooden sculptures depicting Asmat people in the strangest circumstances, such as playing hockey).

While we were talking, a young man approached us: he was Bapak Deki's grandson, Benny. He had been working at the pavilion as a general assistant for several years, and, like Deki, was a carver. As is common with the Asmat, he loved dancing and was a keen drummer. He showed me some of Bapak Deki's works and a hand-drawn portrait of his grandfather displayed behind a miniaturized *mbis* pole.

According to Benny and the lady, Deki had been happy there.[52] However, as Benny explained to me in subsequent talks, although his grandfather was very popular, he had to rely on tips and the sales of his carvings to get by, unlike the employed staff (mainly Javanese and Sulawesi-Bugis or Toraja—but also Indo-Chinese). This situation deeply frustrated Deki, and he referred to the employees by their ethnicities, which are also those Indonesian ethnic groups that are most represented in Papua and West Papua provinces. Benny said:

> If people tried to ask something to Tete Deki, he wouldn't reply. . . . He wouldn't because he used to say, "I'm not paid [to do that]! I have to work hard to earn my meal!" He had such a strong character! One day something similar occurred: a friend of mine from the campus starts to ask grandpa Deki about Papua, what's in there, and so on. Deki doesn't like it, and he chases us away, he chases us away with a stone ax! And he grasps his spear, huh! "You know that! Never do it with me! Always with the same person, why not to Toraja people! I am the one who is not paid here!" he says. He got so angry at that time, grandpa Deki. . . . "If you want to know about Papua, what is in Papua there, go and talk to the Chinese people, don't do it with me again, I'm not paid here!" Now, it's been a long time. . . . If Papua [Pemda Papua] had given a salary, he would have been keen to explain this, this, this and that![53]

[51] "*Asmat dan Kamoro seni sama, mereka seperti kakak.*"

[52] "*Dia sangat senang.*"

[53] "*Kalau orang minta Tete Deki apa itu, dia tidak mau . . . Orangnya tidak mau, karena dia, omongnya begini 'Jangan sama saya, sama orang ini aja, karena saya tak lebih digaji di sini, saya cari makan sendiri!' Susah orangnya! Waktu dulu sama teman saya orang sekolah kampus, omong sama Tete Deki tentang Papua, di Papua ada apa . . . Dia tidak suka, dia kejar, pake kampak kejar, tombak, wa! 'Tahu jangan sama saya! Sama orang, kan Toraja! Saya orang nggak digaji di sini!' kata dia. Dia marah di situ. Tete Deki . . . 'Kalau kamu mau tahu mengenai Papua, yang di Papua sana, sama orang Cina aja, jangan sama saya, saya di sini tidak digaji!' Sekarang udah lama kelamaan . . . Udah jika di Papua sini kasih gaji, baru dia mau! Mau juga, jelas ini, ini, ini, itu.*"

Benny also spoke about the unease Deki experienced and the hierarchical setting typical of the New Order that he had come up against:

> Bapak Deki said [to the shop owner], "Lady, if someone wants to talk to me, say that the person [Deki] does not want to, or rather this person here isn't given a salary for this task or similar" protests Deki. However, the lady forgets Deki's recommendation, and she eventually calls him again: "Deki, some guests want to talk to you!" "What? You should already know! I already told you!!! I am not receiving a salary for this! If people come here and want to ask for this and that, it is not possible!" Oh, Grandpa got so angry. . . . And grasped his spear![54]

I talked further with Benny about the work of cultural and artistic homogenization in the park, as the display and its improbable provincial blends demonstrated.

Benny told me that diversity should be preserved and not blended as in the pavilion's museum ("in the museum, everything is mixed up"),[55] as he felt that Papuan cultures are very different ("if you take people from Jayapura, [the] culture is extremely different").[56] He claimed that it was not right to homogenize cultural traditions ("much more people like Asmat")[57] or to give more importance to some cultures based on their administrative rank, as in the case of the Tobati-Enggros ethnic group indigenous of the Jayapura Regency (the capital of the Papua province). In the end, as he emphasized, the pavilion is paid for by all Papuan people ("Who pays? Local government, the Governor, not Taman Mini. . . . Everything here is paid by Papua").[58]

We also discussed with Benny the Papuan and Asmat image projected through the pavilion to the external world. As analyzed in more detail in another paper, Benny confirmed that the image of primitiveness is what visitors to the Papua Pavilion expect.[59] He adapted to it, and, in his performance, he usually plays the role of the primitive man wearing a variety of Papuan decorations and giving the stereotypical ululating war cry of Native Americans. During my visits to the Asmat Pavilion, he seemed to enjoy performing the role, and probably humoring visitors' expectations by playing the image of the primitive. Although he was not explicit about this point, I suspect there might also be some internal amusement in parodying ridiculous stereotypes. But he said to be nevertheless quite surprised at their compulsion to buy souvenirs even when they were

---

[54] "'Ibu, nanti kalau ada orang yang cari saya, bilang orangnya nggak mau, atau orangnya di sini nggak kasih gaji atau nggak bicara sama ibu. Cuma, waktu itu ibu nggak tahu, nggak ingat, dan ibu panggil Tete Deki 'Oh ada tamu, Deki!' 'Kenapa? Kamu kasih tahu! Saya udah bilang! Saya di sini nggak dikasih gaji! Kalau orang mau datang ke sini mau minta penjelasan ini yang buat di Papua [dll.], nggak bisa, orangnya!' Aduh, Tete Deki marah-marah . . . ngamuk-ngamuk! Bawa tombak!"

[55] I refer, for instance, to the idea of selecting for each province one sole trait; for example, a singular song or dance. For the Papuan province (and pavilion) a single dance (*Tarian Musiah*), a traditional weapon (*pisao belati*), and a tune (*Apuse Yamko Tambe Tamka*) have been identified and employed. See Nestu D. Edhi and Mas'ud Thoyib, *Penciptaan Ruang Budaya Untuk Pelindungan, Pengembangan dan Pendidikan Warisan Budaya di Taman Mini Indonesia Indah—Creation of Cultural for Safeguarding, Development, and Education in Cultural Heritage at Beautiful Indonesia in Miniature Park* (Jakarta: Panitia Kegiatan National; Taman Mini "Indonesia Indah," 2012), 95.

[56] "Kalau orang Jayapura, budaya beda-beda."

[57] "Paling banyak suka Asmat."

[58] "Siapa bayar? Pemerintah lokal, Gubernur, bukan Taman Mini . . . Ini bayar oleh Papua semua."

[59] Roberto Costa, "Authentic Primitive Art and Indigenous Global Desires Between Reality and Hyperreality," *The Journal of Transcultural Studies* 10, no. 2 (2019): 194–214.

Figure 7. Benny posing with a park visitor. (Papua Pavilion, Taman Mini, 2018)

not properly refined: once, he was chiseling an object that was not finished, but the shop owner insisted on selling it nonetheless. "Ah, don't worry, that's because it's authentic," the shop owner said.[60] This speaks volumes on the place of Asmat art in the imagination of international but also Indonesian people who believe that specific features such as roughness and unfinishedness are the essential traits to discriminate authentic from fake "primitive" art.

During our talks, Benny demonstrated to be a lighthearted and cheerful man and nonchalantly recounted his anecdotes and offered his opinions. Above all, he loved being in contact with people and sharing elements of Asmat/Papuan culture. At the time of this visit, as he disclosed to me with great excitement, he was busy with a new project: the erection of an Asmat men's house (*jeuw*). Indeed, in addition to a plan for the pavilion that foresees the building of a two-story café and a new art shop as well as the restoration of the Dani village to better depict authentic traditions, he planned to work on the construction of the Asmat architectural blueprint and sociopolitical center of each village, which is known as the *jeuw*. It is in the *jeuw* that moieties and diverse clans gather, discuss, and make important decisions, young people are trained to the customs, and the whole village celebrates traditional festivals and honors their ancestors. Benny explained his project:

> There is a restoration plan next year. By that time, all buildings will be demolished and erected from scratch, like the Dani village: it has to be made of stone to make it steady from the ground so that the stones hold the walls. That's the original way. Everything will be renovated. Later there will also be the traditional Asmat house, the *jeuw* that will be erected here too. Just in front of it, there will be a

---

[60] "'Ah, bukan, itu karena asli' kata dia."

mbis pole [ancestor pole]. . . . I will work [carve] inside next year . . . because my boss wants me to make a layout to build a *jeuw*. I said, "Boss, I can't make a *jeuw* without raising it off the ground with stilts: if you build it directly on the ground, Asmat people can get angry with me. It is not possible! Special wood should be used, and there should be a porch. . . ." "So, what do you want to put first, what is more important?" the boss asks. "Everything, boss!" I reply. There will be silkworm feasts, sago feasts; there will be too. . . . That's correct! With fire to roast . . . there will be a stream of callers! Then with masks [*Jipae* feast], at the very end . . . from house to house . . . sago, fish . . . like that. And with its traditional song—"*Datu, yaya/ mané, ena/ sefaiya afama/ jimu tapinisia/ ay waya/ say woo/ oooooo*"—spirits are in the *jeuw*. There are spirits in those masks. I will make the *jeuw* according to the original way; it is prohibited to build it straightaway [without those ceremonies] . . . because I am an Asmat! "Just make it original" the boss said. I'll take friends from Lenteng Agung and the many young Asmat who study at University. They also know how to build a *jeuw*.[61]

This renovation plan brought fresh energy to Benny: demolishing and rebuilding sounded like a kind of liberation to him, especially when he detailed the replacement of concrete with authentic materials. His enthusiasm increased when he mentioned the construction of the *jeuw*. For him, building a *jeuw* means having a piece of Asmat in the place where he works: it is in the *jeuw* that he can carve, perform traditional ceremonies and feasts, and receive spiritual forces. Moreover, this construction will rebalance the ethnic architectural display of the pavilion—wherein Asmat is underrepresented—while providing a strong and iconic sign to manifest his pride in being Asmat ("I am Asmat"). His enthusiasm was further boosted by the possibility of involving the Asmat diaspora in Jakarta, not just in an occasional informal gathering but in a powerful expression of Asmat agency.

The Allure of Tradition

Benny's desire for building a *jeuw* aims to heighten the Asmat status among other Papuan ethnic groups. Thus, this project is intended to contrast the motley representation of pan-Papuan-ness in the pavilion that, as discussed above, epitomizes the regional expression of Indonesian cultural identity.[62] However, building such a *jeuw* can also presuppose adhering to the logic of cultural homogenization inherent to the park. Indeed the projected *jeuw* will not be the expression of a particular village group and will not

---

[61] "*Ada rencana renovasi tahun depan. Tadi renovasi semua, dibongkar, bikin baru, ini rumah suku Dani, maka begini, Cuma hasil dia camping ini, dan depan harus dari batu, buat tahan di bawa ini batu-batu kasih dinding, aslinya. Renovasi semua. Nanti ada rumah suku Asmat, rumah jeuw, taruh di sini juga. Nanti di depan ada patung mbis. . . . Saya kerja di dalam itu tahun depan . . . karena bos saya dia mau saya bikin gambar buat rumah jeuw. Saya bilang 'Bos, tidak boleh taruh di bawah, tanpa tiang: kalau di bawah, begini, orang Asmat marah sama saya'. Tidak boleh! Harus kayu khusus, dan ada serambi. . . ." Dia panjangnya segini, lebar. "Jadi kamu mau taruh utama apa lagi" katanya." "Semua ini, bos" saya jawab. Ada pesta ulat sagu, pesta sagu, ada . . . Itu benar! Pake api bakar, lari sini! Nanti pake sarung setan, terakhir . . . ke rumah-rumah . . . sagu, ikan . . . begitu. Nyanyinya "Datu, yaya, mané, ena sefaiya afama jimu tapinisia ay waya/ say waya/ oooo." Jadi setan dalam rumah jeuw. Itu roh, itu. Pake barang itu, kah. Saya bikin rumah aslinya, tidak boleh ini langsung . . . karena saya orang Asmat. "Bikin asli aja," bos katanya . . . Nanti ambil teman-teman dari Lenteng Agung, anak-anak Asmat yang kuliah banyak. Tapi mereka tahu bikin rumah juga.*"

[62] See Michael Cookson, "Batik Irian: Imprints of Indonesian Papua" (PhD diss., Australian National University, 2008), 237–336.

be linked to the spirit world, as one would expect from an authentic *jeuw*. Rather, it will represent an ideal *jeuw* of all Asmat people: a pan-Asmat customary house replica.

The striking paradox of this project is that it attempts to redress the consolidated hierarchies and structural inequalities present in the pavilion's exhibition by employing the same idiom and logic that underlie the park's conceptualization. A pan-Asmat *jeuw* is indeed seen by Benny as a heuristic solution to oppose, not unambiguously, the assimilation of Asmat identity to pan-Papuan-ness. This opposition is therefore nothing but the reiteration of the same logical pattern featured in the park, but repeated on a smaller scale. Such a phenomenon is what Gal has termed "fractal recursivity," that is, "a distinction . . . co-constitutive . . . which can be reproduced repeatedly by projecting it onto narrower and broader comparisons."[63] It follows that the foundational logic of the park, which triggers the compulsion for tradition within the provincial clusters, now fuels a similar search for authentic traditions within smaller administrative units, the regencies.

On the one hand, the *jeuw* project seems to confirm the endurance of certain patterns of the New Order's cultural politics in the post-Suharto era, which can be observed within the park, but also outside of it: see, for example, the emergence of new regencies that mushroom across Indonesia and in Papua in particular. This administrative fragmentation in turn creates new local leaders who are occasionally dubbed by the press as "mini-Suhartos," replicating authoritative leadership patterns at a local level, and gives rise to new cultural identities coinciding with the regency enclosures.

On the other hand, the project also shows the difficulty of escaping the "power of Mini-ization." The appeal of ordered and stable cultural systems, even when the change is driven by a genuine search for cultural authenticity, is considerable. The formulation of projects that may have an empowering value can therefore easily fall into the standards set by the park's chronotopic setting. As a result, the response to an enthusiastic project may lead to new fractal recursive instances that, like in a matryoshka doll, can be repeated *ad infinitum*.

Metamorphoses in an Everlasting Present?

For those people, as the Papuans, who have been obliged to fit "the national narrative of ethnicity—*Bhinneka Tunggal Ika*—and the narrative of international tourism—the romance of first encounter in a 'Stone Age' land," any change can be a significant source of hope and enthusiasm.[64] Whether these changes can mark a rupture with certain imaginaries typical of the hierarchical and atemporal setting of the park is, however, a separate discourse. That is what this analysis has attempted to explore.

The project of the pan-Asmat *jeuw*, which is the centerpiece of my analysis, reveals indeed a precise kind of change: to allow Asmat people to occupy a more meaningful space in the pavilion and the park's space while dignifying Benny's fellow Asmat and their cultural heritage. Consequently, such a project is expected

---

[63] Susan Gal, "Language Ideologies Compared: Metaphors of Public/Private," *Journal of Linguistic Anthropology* 15, no. 1 (2005): 26–27.

[64] Danilyn Rutherford, "Of Birds and Gifts: Reviving Tradition on an Indonesian Frontier," *Cultural Anthropology* 11 (1996): 583.

to restore Asmat pride by bringing Asmat people to the same level as other Papuan (and Indonesian) ethnic groups.

As argued, though, all these plans and aspirations for actual metamorphoses, rather than destabilizing old political paradigms and structural inequalities, instead reinforce them. The projected edification of a *jeuw* of all Asmat can indeed be regarded as an act that indexes a process of cultural reproduction, in Pemberton's words, "Mini-ization." Thus, despite the genuine intentions of Benny, this *jeuw* will be a replica detached from its authentic spiritual value and will represent a supplementary example of homogenization and reductionism in the pavilion, although probably somewhat more authentic than other customary houses in its appearance. Ahistoricity and cultural standardization will plunge this new simulacrum into the park's everlasting present in order to further foster the Stone Age romance of Papuans and Asmat people.

Given this scenario, and reconsidering my research questions, I am inclined to think that the New Order's cultural discourse and its compulsion for culture are still extant in Taman Mini—and beyond its enclosure. It is indeed its replicability that enlivens the spirit or *sakti* of the New Order, which is also preserved in the park's peculiar spatiotemporality.[65] Further analyses on Taman Mini are therefore expected to show how reformative initiatives taking place in such marginal pavilions as the Papua Pavilion will progress, and to what extent the aspirations for change can destabilize the park's (and nation's) enduring compulsion for tradition and its replicability.

---

[65] *Sakti* is the Javanese indigenous concept of "power."

Indonesian Student Theses on "1965": An Overview

Grace Leksana and Douglas Kammen

Over the past two decades, there has been an enormous outpouring of scholarship on "1965"—a common and convenient, though oftentimes misleading, shorthand for the political events of October 1 of that year and the massive violence unleashed against the political Left over the next few years in Indonesia. Across this terrain, research by foreign scholars has been particularly prominent. This has included major monographs by Victor Fic (*Anatomy of the Jakarta Coup: October 1, 1965*, 2005), John Roosa (*Pretext for Mass Murder: The September 30th Movement and Suharto's Coup d'Etat in Indonesia*, 2006), Vannessa Hearman (*Unmarked Graves: Death and Survival in the Anti-Communist Violence in East Java, Indonesia*, 2018), Geoffrey Robinson (*The Killing Season: A History of the Indonesian Massacres, 1965–66*, 2018), Jess Melvin (*The Army and the Indonesian Genocide: Mechanics of Mass Murder*, 2018), Saskia Wieringa and Nursyahbani Katjasungkana (*Propaganda and the Genocide in Indonesia: Imagined Evil*, 2020), Vincent Bevins (*The Jakarta Method: Washington's Anticommunist Crusade and the Mass Murder Program that Shaped Our World*, 2020), and John Roosa (*Buried Histories: The Anticommunist Massacres of 1965–1966 in Indonesia*, 2020); edited volumes by Douglas Kammen and Katharine McGregor (*The Contours of Mass Violence in Indonesia, 1965–68*, 2012) and Katharine McGregor, Jess Melvin, and Annie Pohlman (*The Indonesian Genocide of 1965: Causes, Dynamics and Legacies*, 2018); and a huge number of journal articles and book chapters. Since 1998, the output and visibility of Indonesian scholars writing on 1965 also increased dramatically, with major books by Hermawan Sulistyo (*Palu Arit di Ladang Tebu*, 2000), Harsutejo (*G30S: Sejarah yang Digelapkan*, 2003), John Roosa, Ayu Ratih, and Hilmar

Grace Leksana is a lecturer at the Department of History, State University of Malang (Universitas Negeri Malang) in Indonesia; and Douglas Kammen is Associate Professor and Dean's Chair in the Department of Southeast Asian Studies at the National University of Singapore.

Farid (*Tahun yang Tak Pernah Berakhir*, 2004), I Ngurah Suryawan (*Ladang Hitam di Pulau Dewata*, 2007), Baskara Wardaya (*Truth Will Out*, 2009), Asvi Warman Adam (*Melawan Lupa, Menepis Stigma*, 2006, and *1965: Orang-orang di Balik Tragedi*, 2009), Amurwani Dwi Lestariningsih (*Gerwani: Kisah Tapol Wanit di Kamp Plantungan*, 2011), as well as a number of memoirs. Alongside these published works by scholars working both in and outside of Indonesia, there is a third stream of scholarship that, while rarely noted, is deserving of our attention: the growing number of BA, MA, and PhD theses written by students at Indonesian universities.

The proliferation of Indonesian scholarship on 1965 has not taken place in a political vacuum, of course. The end of Suharto's New Order regime in 1998 opened the floodgates of this new scholarship, but the specter of communism and the long-defunct Communist Party of Indonesia (*Partai Komunis Indonesia*, PKI) remain alive and continue to haunt local and national politics.[1] Anticommunist banners appeared in various locations in rural Java in the early 2000s. Anticommunist demonstrators have threatened gatherings of former political prisoners. And national politicians periodically have expressed outrage over the publication of books by the children of PKI members (e.g., Ribka Tjiptaning's *Aku Bangga Jadi Anak PKI*, 2002). During the 2014 presidential election, supporters of former general and Suharto's son-in-law Prabowo Subianto spread accusations that candidate Joko Widodo's father was Chinese and that the family was affiliated with the PKI. Five years later, once again running for the presidency, Subianto charged that President Widodo had a "Boyolali mug" (*tampang Boyolali*), implying that Widodo was a coarse village upstart, and indirectly linking the president to a district in which the PKI enjoyed particular strength up until 1965. Soon after, an Islamic organization in Makassar conducted a sweep of the Gramedia bookstore and seized books about the PKI and communism. These may appear to be isolated incidents, but together are part of a recurrent leitmotif of military and Islamic politics in post-Suharto Indonesia. The bogeyman of communism retains its power to intimidate, and perhaps more importantly to draw lines and consolidate constituencies. It is within this context of postauthoritarian openness in the realms of research, publishing, and heightened political polarization that the proliferation of student theses about 1965 must be seen.

This review aims to survey the growth of Indonesian student theses about the mass violence of the mid-1960s (including its antecedents and long-term consequences), to highlight the distribution of topics covered over time, and to offer some modest suggestions for future research. To capture the rise of interest among Indonesian university students in the history of 1965, we compiled a list of more than three hundred theses (mostly BA theses, but also a smaller number of MA theses and a handful of PhD dissertations) produced between 1970 and 2019 about 1965. For practical reasons, we limit the scope to universities on the island of Java. We have relied almost entirely on digital university repositories and internet searches. It goes without saying that this is by no means a comprehensive collection, but we believe the coverage is sufficient to provide a bird's eye view of the field. The data set includes the author's name, the thesis title, the university, the degree for which the thesis was written, the student's department, and the year of completion. We have categorized these along two dimensions: a dozen

---

[1] See, for example, Stephen Miller, "Zombie Anti-Communism? Democratization and the Demons of Suharto-Era Politics in Contemporary Indonesia," in *The Indonesian Genocide of 1965*, eds. Katharine McGregor, Jess Melvin, and Annie Pohlman (Cham, Switzerland: Palgrave Macmillan, 2018), 287–310.

general categories including political actors, historical background, violence, memory, media studies, etc.; and theses that are general or national in scope versus those that are focused on a particular locality. Throughout the review, we use the label "1965" as shorthand for the universe of cases that examine the antecedents to, events and dynamics of, and legacies resulting from the destruction of the Indonesian Communist Party in 1965–66.

Breaching the Taboo

Under Suharto's three decades of rule, the state closely controlled information, media reporting, and public discussion about 1965. The official line was that the Indonesian Communist Party masterminded the September 30th Movement and intended to use it to seize power; that the army took decisive action to safeguard the nation; and that so-called nationalist and religious groups took decisive action to combat the communist menace. This interpretation was presented in army publications, repeated by state officials, obediently reproduced in the media, and taught to children in schools. September was dubbed anticommunist month and included mandatory screenings of the propaganda film *Pengkhianatan G30S/PKI* (*The Treachery of G30S/PKI*) in all schools together with red scare campaigns in which children were encouraged to search for and report on communist symbols (in magazines, on t-shirts, and even hidden in camouflage clothing), the discovery of which proved the latent presence of *ekstrim kiri* (the extreme Left, i.e., communists).

In this context, it was only natural for university professors to steer clear of any serious discussion of the mass violence on which the New Order was founded. They did so for their own safety as well as to protect their students. But there were occasional exceptions. In the 1970s and 1980s, a few students at elite universities received permission to write theses that touched on the events of 1965. The topics that received approval were overwhelmingly concerned with macropolitics—the struggle over national leadership, Indonesia's foreign relations, the history of student activism, and the adaptation of long-term political prisoners after their release. The only thesis written during the 1970s and 1980s that directly addressed the violence against the Left did so from the perspective of the role played by members of a rural Islamic school (*pesantren*) rather than that of the victims.[2] In the 1990s, the number of student theses on 1965 increased fourfold over the previous decade, though this probably says more about particular professors and the political positioning of specific universities (the University of Indonesia in Jakarta/Depok, Universitas Islam Negeri Sunan Ampel in Surabaya, and Gadjah Mada University in Yogyakarta) than it does about the overall level of student interest in the history of communism in Indonesia or the founding violence of the New Order.[3] As was the case in the 1980s, the only theses that focused on violence were framed in terms of the role played by Islamic organizations or student groups against the Left.

[2] Yusron Hasani, "Partisipasi Pesantren Tempurejo Walikukun dalam Penumpasan G30S/PKI di Ngawi" (bachelor's thesis, Universitas Islam Negeri Sunan Ampel, Surabaya, 1986).

[3] Although beyond the immediate scope of this essay, it is worth noting Indonesians who have written MA theses and doctoral disserations about 1965 at foreign universities: Iwan Sudjatmiko, Harvard University PhD, 1992; Herman Sulistyo, Arizona State University PhD, 1997; Budiawan, National University of Singapore MA, 2003; Vannessa Hearman, Melbourne University PhD, 2012; Dahlia Setiawan, UCLA PhD, 2014; and Grace Leksana, Leiden University PhD, 2020.

Table 1: Theses about the PKI, 1965, and Mass Violence by Year

	BA	MA	PhD	Unknown	Total
1970–79	2	—	—	—	2
1980–89	6	1	—	—	7
1990–99	19	8	—	1	28
2000–09	59	12	2	—	73
2010–19	176	15	3	—	194
Total	262	36	5	1	304

It comes as no surprise that there was a sharp increase in student interest in the events of 1965 following President Suharto's resignation in 1998. Democratization was accompanied by far greater press freedom. Newspapers and magazines openly reported on past human rights abuses, the initiatives of nongovernmental organizations lobbying on behalf of former political detainees, coverage of new research on the events of 1965–66, the discovery of mass graves, and the fate of former political prisoners. Publishing houses responded to the political opening by reprinting long-banned works by major Leftist figures, bringing out new translations of Marxist works and publishing dozens of books (often in translation) about the year 1965. This outpouring in the media and from book publishers helped prompt greater curiosity among students and a new openness on the part of university professors and administrators about the founding acts of the New Order. With this, the number of theses on 1965 increased to 73 in the first decade of the twenty-first century, and then to 193 in the next decade (see Table 1).

Although the vast majority (85 percent) of theses about 1965 produced after 1998 continued to be written at state universities, there was a significant geographic shift in their location. During the New Order, more than two-thirds of the known theses on 1965 were written at the University of Indonesia; since the year 2000, two-thirds of all theses on 1965 have been written at universities in Central Java, Yogyakarta, and East Java (see Table 2).[4] With this, there has also been diversification in the kinds of universities where the theses are being written—including many second-tier as well as private universities—and the disciplines in which students are majoring.

Theses by Topic

Of greatest interest are the topics on which university students have written theses and how these have shifted over time. For purposes of analysis, we have created fourteen general categories (see Table 3), but must warn that based on titles and synopses alone many theses could be placed in more than one category. Two examples will help illustrate the difficulty of simple classification and the logic that we have employed. A thesis with the title "Nadhlatul Ulama from 1950 to 1965" has been placed in category 1, Political Figures and Parties, while a thesis about conflict between Nadhlatul Ulama and the PKI

---

[4] Outside of Java, there are state universities, such as Sam Ratulangi University in Manado, where students are still not allowed to write theses about communism or the events of 1965.

Table 2: Theses about 1965 by Province where the University Is Located

	Jakarta	West Java[a]	Banten	Central Java	Yogya	East Java	Total
1970–79	2	—	—	—	—	—	2
1980–89	4	1	—	—	—	2	7
1990–99[b]	1	15	—	—	6	5	27
2000–09	6	17	—	11	20	19	73
2010–19	31	29	1	28	29	76	194
Total	44	62	1	39	55	102	303

[a]Many of the theses listed under West Java were written at Universitas Indonesia, which relocated to Depok in 1987, so should in fact be treated as part of the greater Jakarta region: one in the late 1980s, eleven in the 1990s, thirteen in the 2000s, and thirteen in the 2010s.

[b]One thesis for which the university is unknown.

from 1960 until 1965 has been listed under category 5, Politics Prior to October 1, 1965. In another instance of overlap, a thesis about the student movement in the founding of the New Order has been classified under category 8, Student Movement, while a thesis about the Indonesian University Student Action Front (*Kesatuan Aksi Mahasiswa Indonesia*, KAMI) has been classified under category 9, Dynamics of Violence. Given the overlap and somewhat arbitrary nature of the classifications, the reader is advised to view the data in clusters (from left to right) that cover politics and the Left prior to 1965 (topics 1–6), the production of violence following the events of October 1, 1965 (topics 3 and 7–9), the consequences of the destruction of the PKI for victims and broader identities (topics 10–12), and theses that highlight representation of 1965 in the arts and media (topics 12–14).

In the 1970s and 1980s, as we have already noted, the few theses about 1965 focused on the overthrow of Sukarno and the founding of Suharto's regime. In the 1990s, a growing number of student theses directly addressed the reasons for and dynamics of violence, with particular interest shown in the unilateral land actions carried out by the Indonesian Peasant Union (*Barisan Tani Indonesia*) in 1963–64 and the role played by the army's civilian allies—the "religious" and "nationalist" groups—in the mass arrests and killings initiated after October 1, 1965. A formulaic title emerged during this period: "The Role of Actor X in the Destruction of the PKI in Location Y" (*Peranan X dalam penumpasan PKI di Kabupaten Y*). Initially the tenor of these theses was approving, if not outright celebratory; but by the 1990s there was the odd student or two who subverted the formula to question the state's orthodoxy, either by highlighting the subordination of civilians to the military or by arguing that truth-seeking was a necessary step toward making amends with the victims.

The distribution of thesis topics becomes of real interest in the period since Suharto's resignation. At the aggregate level, the most significant developments can be summarized by decade. In the first decade of the twenty-first century, there was a sharp increase in the number of theses written about the history of Indonesian communism (the PKI, its leaders, its affiliated organizations, and conflicts with other parties both before and after 1965), and, depending on theoretical perspective and taste, topics concerned with

Table 3: BA, MA, and PhD Theses about 1965 by Topic

Decade	Figures, Parties, IR	PKI and Affiliates	Indonesian Military	1926 and 1948 Rebellions	Pre-Oct. 1965 Politics	Agrarian Conflict	Sept. 30 Movement	Student Movement	Dynamics of Violence	Survivors, Human Rights	Sociocultural Impacts	Memory and History	Arts, Literature, Film	Media Studies of 1965	Totals
1970–79	—	—	1	—	—	—	—	1	—	—	—	—	—	—	2
1980–89	3	—	1	—	1	—	—	—	1	1	—	—	—	—	7
1990–99	4	3	—	1	4	2	—	3	6	1	1	2	1	—	28
2000–09	7	13	6	3	9	3	2	—	13	9	5	3	—	—	73
2010–19	11	19	2	6	16	9	4	5	21	18	19	10	38	15	193
Total	25	35	10	10	30	14	6	9	41	29	25	15	39	15	303

victims or survivors (their experiences in prison, stigmatization after release, and human rights). In the 2010s, by contrast, the most prominent development was an outpouring of works on memory, debates over the writing and teaching of history, literature, and arts (roughly 30 percent), together with the rise of media studies of how the year 1965 is reported and debated in post-Suharto Indonesia.

Local Studies

While the distribution of BA, MA, and PhD theses by topic reveals how student interest has developed over time, it fails to capture one of the most significant dimensions of the outpouring of recent interest in 1965: the distinction between theses that adopt a national or macrolevel approach and those that focus on a particular locality (usually a city or district, but in some cases an entire province). During the New Order, only one-third of all theses about 1965 focused on a particular locality; in the decade from 2000 to 2009 this rose to half; and for the period between 2010 and 2019 this declined slightly to 40 percent. Of greater interest is the geographic distribution of these local studies. We have not found a single study of the PKI or the events of 1965 set in Jakarta and only seven local studies on the topic for all of West Java, and these mostly skirt the question of violence, focusing instead on issues like political figures, pre-1965 politics, and post-1965 sociocultural dynamics. While it is certainly true that levels of detention and killings were far lower in West Java than in Central and East Java (as well as in Bali and North Sumatra), there is still something disconcerting about the relative lack of interest in the political conflicts that led up to October 1965, in the dynamics of violence, and in the consequences in Jakarta and West Java. Why, one might ask, have students not thought to study the grassroots mobilization in Jakarta in early October 1965, detention centers such as Salemba and Bukit Duri, or the struggles of former Leftists and ex-political prisoners in specific neighborhoods? Similarly, one wonders why students have not explored dynamics in the parts of West Java where violence was intense (such as the Subang–Indramayu–Cirebon belt), or examined the response of Muslim groups in former Darul Islam strongholds (especially Garut and Tasikmalaya) or Banten?

While there has been a significant uptick in theses that examine particular localities in Central Java and Yogyakarta, there are notable differences between the two. More than two-thirds of theses about Central Java are local, but these are overwhelmingly about the Surakarta and Salatiga residencies and the city of Semarang; the western half of the province—Kedu, Banyumas, and the north coast stretch from Tegal to Pekalongan—is grossly underrepresented. In Yogyakarta, by contrast, only six out of fifty-five theses (11 percent) are local in nature, and none focus on the production or dynamics of violence; instead, the topics are survivors, memory and history, and sociocultural legacies. Of greatest interest is East Java, where local studies account for 80 percent of all student theses. Remarkably, theses are evenly distributed across all four of the Subregional Military Commands (Korem). That distribution has been driven in part by well-known cases: nine theses about the 1948 communist uprising in Madiun (Korem 081), eight theses about the anticommunist violence in the Kediri–Jombang region (Korem 082), seven theses about the outbreak of large-scale violence in Banyuwangi in October 1965, seven theses about the operations against PKI remnants in Blitar in 1967–68 (Korem 083), along with a cluster of theses focused on the greater Surabaya region (Korem 084).

Table 4: Location-Specific Theses about the PKI/1965 by Province

	Jakarta	West Java	Central Java	Yogya	East Java	Outside Java	Total
1970–79	—	—	—	—	—	—	—
1980–89	—	1	—	—	2	—	3
1990–99	—	2	—	—	7	—	9
2000–09	—	—	12	1	23	—	36
2010–19	—	4	16	5	51	2*	78
Total	—	7	28	6	83	2	126

*One thesis about military operations against communists in Bali in 1965–66 and one thesis about the 1965 law on religion in Lombok.

Although not strictly a geographic issue, the contrast between Central Java/ Yogyakarta and East Java helps reveal a deeper divide: ideological contestation. Universitas Islam Negeri Sunan Ampel, located in Surabaya, East Java, has been ground zero for scholarship that celebrates the role of Islamic organizations—especially Nadhlatul Ulama and its paramilitary wing Ansor, but also student groups, individual Islamic teachers (*kyai*), and their schools (*pesantren*)—in the destruction of the PKI and the salvation of the nation. This is by no means a new phenomenon, but the increase in such theses must be viewed as a reaction to the post-1998 call for a truth commission tasked with investigating human rights abuses committed in (and after) 1965–66 and the widespread media coverage and (re)publication of Leftist books that ensued. This reaction was by no means uniform, with many Islamic campuses deeply divided in terms of their approach to the study of history and engagement in Indonesia's new democratic politics. The anticommunist wing, and particularly those who traced their positions to Masjumi and the Islamic University Student Union (*Himpunan Mahasiswa Islam*), received a major boost from the appearance of new scholarship reinterpreting Indonesian history through an Islamic lens. Within this genre, Ahmad Mansur Suryanegara's two-volume *Api Sejarah* (2009 and 2011) is the most serious and far and away the most influential.[5] The counterpoint to pro-Ansor and anticommunist theses at UIN campuses has come from private Catholic universities, especially Universitas Sanata Dharma in Yogyakarta, but also Universitas Katholik Soegijapranoto in Semarang and Universitas Petra in Surabaya, where student theses have tended to focus on human rights and the experiences of former political prisoners, as well as questions of memory and the writing and teaching of history.

---

[5] This is also reflected in the emergence of recent books explicitly attacking communism and the PKI: Saleh As'ad Djamhari et al., *Komunisme di Indonesia* [*Communism in Indonesia*] (Jakarta: Pusjarah and Yayasan Kajian Citra Bangsa, 2009); H. Abdul Mu'nim D.Z., ed., *Benturan NU-PKI 1948–1965* [*The Collision of NU and the PKI, 1948–1965*] (Jakarta: PBUNU, 2013); M. Rizal Fadillah, *Bau Amis Komunis* [*The Stench of Communism*] (Bandung: Lekkas, 2020); and Anab Afifi and Thowaf Zuharon's *Banjir Darah: Kisah Nyata Aksi PKI terhadap Kiai, Santri dan Kaum Muslimin* [*Bloodbath: The True Story of PKI Actions against Kiai, Santri and Muslims*] (Solo: Istanbul, 2020).

Discussion and Recommendations for Future Research

The requirement that all undergraduates write a senior thesis is onerous and unnecessarily extends the time to graduation, and at its worst places students at the whims of professors and deans who are eager to wield their authority and even engage in extortion. But as long as the requirement remains in place, undergraduates at Indonesian universities will continue to search for topics about which they care and wish to learn more. With this in mind, we want to offer some thoughts on directions for future student research on the year 1965.

By all appearances, the starting point for many students who write theses about 1965 is a matter of available sources. Perhaps most commonly this will be a book or journal article, but might also be a film, or even family stories. It is essential for students to look beyond the secondary literature and think creatively about primary sources that will provide new points of access, new perspectives, and most importantly raise new questions. Indonesian mass media, and especially newspapers, is conspicuously underrepresented in the three hundred theses we have collected. Several theses explore Leftist newspapers prior to 1965, but only one thesis has made the army's own newspapers the centerpiece of analysis.[6] While it is true that the army closed many newspapers in early October 1965 and tightly controlled what was published thereafter, there is much to be learned from the press, and in particular regional newspapers. Students can consult Roger Paget's helpful listing of Indonesia newspapers published between 1965 and 1967.[7] Many of these are available at the National Library in Jakarta, and some may be found in provincial libraries in Bandung, Semarang, and Surabaya (as well as in provinces beyond Java). A smaller selection are now available online through the Center for Research Libraries.[8] Students might also make greater use of official publications and documentation. Searches of provincial and even district libraries might turn up books, pamphlets, and other ephemera directly relevant to the events of 1965 as well as works by government departments of labor, agriculture, land titling, and the state statistical agency (Bada Pusat Statistik). Beyond written sources, energetic studies might also make greater use of interviews and oral history. While the passage of time has thinned the ranks of direct witnesses to the events of 1965–66, interviews with retired officials, former village heads, and families who lost members can provide windows into the lived experience of the time and the legacies that it left. Along another track, students might consider delving into competing oral accounts of the same event, or events, in a single location.

The second area in which students wishing to conduct research on 1965 can benefit is in what political scientists somewhat annoyingly refer to as "case selection." This is especially true of the selection of localities to be studied. As Table 4 indicates in broad strokes, only since the end of the New Order have Indonesian students (as well as foreign scholars) begun to pay serious attention to the local dynamics of the mass violence against the political Left in the 1960s. But even in Central and East Java, where the

---

[6] Arif Pradono, "Sang Bayi Sudah Mati (Rekayasa Persetujuan Penghancuran PKI di *Harian Berita Yudha* (1965))" (master's thesis, Paramadina University, 2013).

[7] Roger K. Paget, "Indonesian Newspapers 1965–1967," *Indonesia* 4 (October 1967): 170–210.

[8] Available at https://www.crl.edu/.

greatest number of local studies have been conducted, there is still a strong tendency to write about relatively well-known regions—Semarang and the greater Surakarta region (*karesidenan* Surakarta) in Central Java, and Madiun, Kediri, Situbondo, and Blitar in East Java. Many parts of Java remain neglected. West Java is still a terra nullis. While the level of killings was undoubtedly far lower there than elsewhere, there is a desperate need for studies of the Cirebon–Indramayu–Subang stretch along the north coast, of Banten in the west, and of the Darul Islam strongholds of Garut and Tasikmalaya in the highlands. In Central Java, there is a dearth of studies of the Demak–Kudus–Pati triangle, where we know the Army Para-Commando Regiment (RPKAD) operated, the Pekalongan–Tegal littoral, and virtually all of Banyumas. In East Java, little is known about actors or events in Madura, and far too little is known about the southern districts of Tulungagung, Trenggalek, and Pacitan. Recent demographic scholarship by Siddharth Chandra raises new questions about differential levels of violence in lowland and highland parts of Java and the possibility of flight by Leftists from some regions (particularly Madura, Pasuruan, and Probolinggo), and his curious finding that districts on the south coast of East Java had unexpected gains in population.[9] Attention to Chandra's maps and the geographic distribution of theses already written about specific districts in Table 4 may encourage researchers to move beyond well-trodden ground. Doing so would not only help to fill out the map, but also reveal local dynamics that have been overlooked.[10]

If, to this point, the suggestions for future topics have focused on the actors and actions at the height of the attack on the Left, it is equally important to expand our gaze to the longer-term repercussions of the army's actions, its seizure of the state, and the regime that emerged. The classification system introduced by the Operational Command for the Restoration of Security and Order (*Kopkamtib*) in October 1965 set the stage for the purge of the civil service and security apparatuses. But to date there are no serious examinations of how these purges of real or suspected Leftists were carried out, or the processes by which new recruitment was conducted and these institutions were reconstituted. Public school teachers and the civilian defense force (*Hansip*) are of particular importance, and would make for excellent local studies. Students might also consider shifting their gaze from a particular period in time to diachronic analysis that can capture how the attack on the Left paved the way for the implementation of new policies regarding land and property, the introduction of Green Revolution technologies, and the implementation of family planning, and even transmigration. Some of the groundwork for diachronic studies has been laid by Hilmar Farid's 2005 article "Indonesia's Original Sin," but little has been done to further this agenda.[11]

There is also a need to tackle the question of "what's next?" especially on the issue of reconciliation and the ongoing stigmatization of former Leftists. Despite the vast proliferation of theses on art, literature, and media (including international events such

---

[9] See, for example, "New Findings on the Indonesian Killings of 1965–66," *The Journal of Asian Studies* 76, no. 4 (November 2017): 1059–86, on East Java, and "The Indonesian Killings of 1965–1966: The Case of Central Java," *Critical Asian Studies* 51, no. 3 (July 2019): 307–30.

[10] It goes without saying that students studying at universities in Java might also cast their gaze to other regions. While theses written at universities in Sumatra, Kalimantan, Sulawesi, and elsewhere are beyond the scope of this review, it is important to note that there are state universities that still do not allow students to write theses on the events of 1965.

[11] Hilmar Farid, "Indonesia's Original Sin: Mass Killlings and Capitalist Expansion, 1965–1966," *Inter-Asian Cultural Studies* 6, no. 1 (March 2005): 3–16.

as International People's Tribunal and Joshua Oppenheimer's films[12]) over the past decade, there is a tendency to treat such works as cultural products, while avoiding the uncomfortable issue of how these works contribute to (or perhaps even frustrate) reconciliation efforts. Along a parallel track, students might wish to explore the teaching of history about the year 1965, and perhaps how this compares to other controversial periods in Indonesia's past. While a significant number of theses have been written on 1965 by students majoring in history education (twenty-nine theses), only one directly examines the perceptions of teachers on this controversial topic.

---

[12] The Act of Killing was released in 2012, and The Look of Silence was released in 2014.

Leonard C. Sebastian, Syafiq Hasyim, and Alexander R. Arifianto, eds. *Rising Islamic Conservatism in Indonesia: Islamic Groups and Identity Politics.* London and New York: Routledge, 2021. 230 pp.

Robert W. Hefner

During the first years of the post-Suharto transition in 1998–99, Indonesia witnessed a surge in interreligious communal violence, militia mobilization, and attacks on religious minorities. These events led one of the most distinguished foreign analysts of Muslim Indonesia, Martin van Bruinessen, to speak of a "conservative turn in Indonesian Islam."[1] "The transition from authoritarian to democratic rule in Indonesia," van Bruinessen wrote, "has been accompanied by the apparent decline of the liberal Muslim discourse that was dominant during the 1970s and 1980s and the increasing prominence of Islamist and fundamentalist interpretations of Islam."[2] Although some observers had hoped that the continuing operation of electoral democracy might soften the current's hard edges, the 2016–17 mobilization against the Chinese Christian governor of Jakarta, Basuki Tjahaja Purnomo (commonly known as Ahok), indicated that the movement was growing and threatening democracy and multiconfessional citizenship.[3]

It was against this troubled backdrop that the contributors to *Rising Islamic Conservatism in Indonesia* came together in February 2018 on the campus of the Hidayatullah State Islamic University in Jakarta for a conference on "Understanding the Rise of Islamism in Indonesia." The book's thirteen chapters consist of a thoughtful introduction and an epilogue by the editors, which bookend eleven in-depth case studies of Muslim politics and Islamism in contemporary Indonesia. The case studies are written from diverse disciplinary perspectives, from social psychology and anthropology to Islamic studies and political science. Rather than blurring the book's focus, the chapters' multidisciplinary breadth only adds to the book's achievement. No less significant, although two of the three editors are based at the Rajaratnam School of International Studies at Nanyang Technological University, the other twelve contributors are based at public and Islamic universities in Indonesia. These contributions bear witness to the remarkable quality and breadth of scholarship on Islam in Indonesia written by Indonesian academics themselves.

The editors' introduction previews the content of the book's chapters and highlights the themes that unite the volume as a whole. The editors emphasize that "the rise of Islamic conservatism poses significant challenges to Indonesia's continued existence as

Robert W. Hefner is a professor of anthropology and global affairs at the Pardee School of Global Studies, Boston University. He can be reached at rhefner@bu.edu.

[1] Martin van Bruinessen, "What Happened to the Smiling Face of Indonesian Islam? Muslim Intellectualism and the Conservative Turn in Post-Suharto Indonesia" (working paper 222, S. Rajaratnam School of International Studies, Singapore, 2011), and Martin van Bruinessen, ed., *Contemporary Developments in Indonesian Islam: Explaining the "Conservative Turn"* (Singapore: Institute of Southeast Asian Studies, 2013).

[2] Van Bruinessen, "What Happened to the Smiling Face," ii.

[3] See Greg Fealy and Ronit Ricci, eds., *Contentious Belonging: The Place of Minorities in Indonesia* (Singapore: Institute of Southeast Asian Studies, 2019); Tim Lindsey and Helen Pausacker, eds., *Religion, Law and Intolerance in Indonesia* (London and New York: Routledge, 2016); and Daniel Peterson, *Islam, Blasphemy, and Human Rights in Indonesia: The Trial of Ahok* (London and New York: Routledge, 2020).

Indonesia 111 (April 2021)

a multi-religious state" (2). They also rightly underscore that, although radical groups exacerbate the problem, "conservative Islamic groups often do represent opinions . . . that are broadly popular in Indonesian society" (3). As the book's case studies make clear, the varied conservative currents have different social drivers, but most agree in opposing liberalism, gender equality, and the hermeneutic approaches to scripture and jurisprudence favored in progressive Muslim circles.

In chapter 2, Burhanuddin Muhtadi and Rizka Halida draw on national surveys to explore social psychological factors influencing support for radical Islamism. Over the past several years, and often working with the Australia-based scholars Ed Aspinall and Marcus Mietzner, Muhtadi and Halida have established themselves among the leading survey analysts of Muslim affairs in contemporary Indonesia. In this chapter, the authors demonstrate that socioeconomic factors like income, employment, and education correlate less strongly with support for Islamist radical groups than does depth of identification with Islam (14). Their far-ranging analysis also shows that the Islamic Defenders Front (FPI) is the most broadly supported of radical Islamist groups (20); support for Islamism is stronger among women than men (21); and that a full 27.2 percent of Indonesian Muslims subscribe to worldviews that can be categorized as radical (33).

In chapter 3, the Harvard-trained anthropologist Dadi Darmadi examines growing support for Islamist and neo-Salafist viewpoints in five cities across Indonesia. Darmadi's research found that public schools are one of the most important channels for radical ideological transmission. This is in part because teachers providing state-mandated religious instruction show Islamist sympathies on such topics as state-based shariah (62 percent favor) and Indonesia's Pancasila philosophy (23.4 percent oppose) (42). Darmadi also shows that the intellectual menu among young Islamists has also changed, with such grey-haired pioneers of global Islamism as Sayyid Qutdb and Hassan al-Banna giving way to cute militants like the Hizbut-Tahrir activist Felix Siauw, "whose use of language is simple" (49).

In chapter 4, Irman G. Lanti, Akim, and Windy Dermawan explore the growth of Islamism in West Java, home to 18 percent of Indonesia's population. They highlight the central role of online social media in the propagation of Islamist "new dakwah" (66). The authors also show convincingly that the one mass organization leading efforts to contain Islamism in West Java is Nahdlatul Ulama.

In chapter 5, the renowned young Muhammadiyah intellectual Ahmad Najib Burhani explores the impact of Islamist currents on the modernist Muhammadiyah. Burhani shows that the Muhammadiyah's longstanding commitment to education, health care, orphanages, and women's welfare keeps the organization on a steady keel in terms of program priorities, even as some activists have lent their support to radical causes like the anti-Ahok campaign in the political realm. "Muhammadiyah has worldly and social service tasks to be taken care of," and this inner-worldly pragmatism ensures "the organisation does not live only in [a] discursive or utopic world" (90). This theoretical conclusion is of great relevance well beyond Indonesia.

In chapter 6, Asep M. Iqbal draws deftly on framing analysis in social movement theory to explore the rise of the hardline Garis Lurus ("straight line") movement within Nahdlatul Ulama. Notwithstanding the pluralist (if administratively challenged) legacy of the late Abdurrahman Wahid (1940–2009), Nahdlatul Ulama's socially conservative wing has always been larger than its progressive pluralist wing—a tension the Garis Lurus faction has recognized and exploited. The movement surged to prominence at the NU National Congress in 2015, when one of the movement's founders, Idrus Ramli, challenged the incumbent chairman (Said Aqil Siradj) for the NU executive leadership, calling him a "dumb professor." The Garis Lurus leadership is "young, attractive, and educated" (97), and, like so many Islamist groupings, has skillfully used new social media to circumvent NU hierarchies and appeal directly and often crudely to an impatient online youth.

In chapter 7, Syafiq Hasyim explores the discursive background to Council of Indonesian Ulama (MUI) support for the anti-Ahok campaign, as well as its opposition to non-Muslim leadership in general. Hasyim's chapter builds on his 2014 dissertation at the Free University in Berlin, one of the most important studies of Islamic conservatism conducted in the post-Suharto period. In this chapter Hasyim demonstrates that MUI's rulings have shown remarkable consistency over the past twenty years, especially in their unyielding opposition to religious deviancy and their support for Muslim supremacism in political affairs.

Author of one of the important books on Islamism in post-Suharto Indonesia, Masdar Hilmy in chapter 8 analyzes the ideology and organizational expansion of the transnational Islamist movement Hizbut Tahrir Indonesia (HTI). As with so many of Indonesia's new Islamists, HTI adapted early on to web-based social media, but complemented its online presence with print and mosque-based recruitment campaigns. Although in the aftermath of the anti-Ahok campaign (in which HTI figured prominently) the Jokowi administration banned HTI, Hilmy notes that the organization's base among "mostly well-educated middle-class Muslims from 'secular' campuses" (134) remains active, and has even won grassroots support in some of NU's East Java heartland. He cautions, "HTI activists will continue teaching . . . , only now in a more clandestine way" (143).

One of the most infamous Islamist movements of the post-Suharto period, the Indonesian Mujahidin Council (Majelis Mujahidin Indonesia, MMI), seemed poised in the early 2000s to play a dominant role in the struggle for the implementation of shariah-inspired regional regulations (*perda syariah*) in districts and towns across Indonesia. In an incisive historical overview, M. Iqbal Anhaf explores just how factional infighting between the MMI's spiritual leader, Abu Bakar Ba'asyir, and the Yogyakarta-based national executive weakened the organization after 2008. Having pioneered Islamist propaganda in print media, the MMI also never developed an effective online presence. Notwithstanding its decline, the MMI developed (and according to my interviews, still maintains) close ties with the al-Qa'eda–linked Jabhah al-Nusrah movement in Syria.

In the early 2000s, Yon Machmudi carried out the most extensive research ever on Indonesia's *tarbiyah* ("education and moral development") movement, out of which the Prosperous Justice Party (PKS) later emerged. In chapter 10, Machmudi provides a comprehensive update on his earlier study. He explores the impact of Muhammadiyah efforts to curb PKS influence in its ranks. He also shows that there has been a significant ideological shift over the past ten years in the organization—away from the puritanical variety of reform favored by the movement's founders to a more traditionalist theology and social habitus. Sayyid Qutb's radical tracts are no longer studied, and the new leadership "has reintroduced . . . the slogan of the movement that it is the essence of Sufism (*haqiqah sufiyah*)" (172). Machmudi's chapter, too, thus presents a small but notable exception to the general current of growing Islamist conservatism in Indonesia.

If the PKS has softened its Islamist edges, Andar Nubowo in chapter 11 provides an account of the neo-Salafist organization Wahdah Islamiyah (WI). Founded in South Sulawesi in opposition to Suharto-era Pancasila strictures, in recent years the Wahdah Islamiyah has gone national. The organization played a central role in the mobilization against Governor Ahok. The organization's leadership has sought to combine the Muhammadiyah's educational and social service outreach with a neo-Salafi emphasis on "back to the Quran and Sunnah of the Prophet" (193). "Its ideological hybridism and non-confrontational position" indicate that the WI may yet "challenge the long-standing religious authority of Muhammadiyah and NU" (194).

In the volume's final case study (chapter 12), Najib Kailani explores how an important segment of the new Muslim middle class has eschewed confrontational politics in favor of a "market Islam" that combines "a progressive worldview in which Islamic virtues are being taught in a way that complements globalisation and modernity" (199). Kailani takes exception to the portrait of market Islam provided by the French political scientist Patrick Haenni, who has described market Islam as the "other global conservatism" (in addition, that is, to Western neoliberalism).[4] Market Islam in Indonesia builds on a booming publishing industry centered on self-help and business guides. These "focus mainly on how to become financially successful while remaining religiously devout" (202). Not so much a conservative current as an individualizing technology of the self, market Islam in Indonesia "does not mean opposition to modernity or Western market-based ideals; in fact it can go hand in hand with it" (206).

In the volume's concluding chapter, the editors stand back from the case studies and describe the primary features of Muslim politics and culture in contemporary Indonesia. Drawing again on Syafiq Hasyim's recent research, they emphasize that the drive to implement shariah ideals in various social spheres will continue, including in the economy. They also predict, again with good reason, that the polarization of Muslim social groupings seen in the 2014 and 2019 elections will remain a feature of Muslim politics for many years to come.

This is a timely and welcome volume—the best sequel yet to van Bruinessen's earlier books on the conservative turn in Indonesian Islam. Less directly but no less significantly, its case studies by Indonesian authors also bear witness to a not-so-conservative feature of the contemporary Indonesian scene: the rise of a new generation of Indonesian academics carrying out brilliant multidisciplinary research on Islam in Indonesia.

---

[4] See Robert W. Hefner, "Islam, Economic Globalization, and the Blended Ethics of Self," *Bustan: The Middle East Review* 3 (2012): 91–108; and James B. Hoesterey, *Rebranding Islam: Piety, Prosperity and a Self-Help Guru* (Stanford, CA: Stanford University Press, 2016).

Josh Stenberg. *Minority Stages: Sino-Indonesian Performance and Public Display.* Honolulu: University of Hawai'i Press, 2019. 274 pp.

Matthew Isaac Cohen[1]

Indonesian Chinese have played important roles in urban artworlds since at least the beginning of the seventeenth century, when European travelers note public performances of *xiqu* (Chinese opera) in the multiethnic port city of Banten. Chinese communities have patronized and performed art forms from China for centuries, not only various forms of *xiqu* but also *barongsay* (lion dancing), Chinese puppetry, and various musical traditions. Major Chinese holidays such as Chinese New Year, the Lantern Festival, and the Dragon Boat Festival were public celebrations observed by entire cities through boisterous parades, diverse cultural performances, gift-giving, fireworks, and participatory rituals such as pole climbing. Large-scale *xiqu* troupes toured the Dutch Indies and other parts of the *Nanyang* (South Seas) as far back as the 1830s, if not earlier, sponsored by wealthy Chinese businessmen, business associations, and community organizations. Chinese traditions fervently cross-pollinated with indigenous and modern forms in the nineteenth and early twentieth centuries—resulting in a multitude of eclectic hybrids such as the *gambang kromong* of the Betawi cultural area of western Java, a syncretic mix of Chinese string and wind instruments with Sundanese gamelan that accompanied social dancing and folk drama. In the last decades of the nineteenth century, as vital commercial theater and entertainment scenes flourished in urban centers, Chinese entrepreneurs assumed leadership roles as producers and impresarios. A major player was the Surabaya Chinese magnate Yap Gwan Thay, who owned theaters and a number of stores and restaurants; produced balloon shows, magic acts, *topeng* (Javanese masked theatre), Chinese opera (in both Malay and Chinese), and two forms of Malay operetta—*komedi stambul* and *bangsawan*; and manufactured carbonated beverages, pharmaceuticals, and fireworks.[2] During the interwar period, Sino-Malay authors were Indonesia's premier playwrights, contributing scripts for both amateur enactments and professional productions. In the twentieth and twenty-first centuries, Chinese Indonesian entrepreneurs also owned record labels, movie studios, and independent television channels.

Minority Stages: Sino-Indonesian Performance and Public Display situates itself as a "preliminary" (169) study of the diversity of Chinese cultural performance in Indonesia, focusing strategically on a number of key theatrical genres (*xiqu, potehi,* and Chinese spoken-language theater), the well-known tale of the Butterfly Lovers Sampek-Engtay as dramatized in popular theater, amateur performance activities under the auspices of community organizations, and large-scale Sino-Indonesian ritual celebrations. The book is based on extensive fieldwork in a number of Indonesian cities and towns, including the metropolitan city of Bandung and Singkawang, a town in West Kalimantan with a near-majority Chinese population, mostly of Hakka derivation. Published literature and

---

[1] Matthew Isaac Cohen is a professor in dramatic arts at the University of Connecticut. He is currently researching the Dr. Walter Angst and Sir Henry Angest Collection of Indonesian Puppets at Yale University Art Gallery as a material cultural resource for the history of *wayang* in Indonesia.

[2] Matthew Isaac Cohen, "Seorang Pujangga Tioghoa dari Surabaya?" in *Sadur: Sejarah Terjemahan di Indonesia dan Malaysia*, ed. Henri Chambert-Loir (Jakarta: KPG, 2010), 877–91.

the popular press are diligently mined, and reference is also made to YouTube videos and other new media.

Citing the work of Melani Budianta and Ien Ang, the author takes performance as a domain in which "Chineseness," a malleable and indeterminate category of identification, is constantly remade and reshaped (5). Before Indonesian independence, "intra-Chinese divisions" based on language (Hokkien, Teochew, Cantonese, and Hakka being predominant in the archipelago) and the racial categories of "pure" (*singkeh* or *totok*) versus "mixed blood" or "acculturated" (*peranakan*) Chinese were significant distinctions (138). Thus the predominately Hokkien population of Java patronized the *potehi* or glove puppet tradition practiced in the southern Fujian region of China from which most of Java's Chinese population originated. As Java's Chinese were mostly *peranakan*, *potehi* increasingly mixed with Javanese practices, and is today performed largely by non-Chinese people in Indonesian, with only occasional Hokkien expressions.

Stenberg understands the eclectic cultural blends of the late colonial period produced by *peranakan* artists as products of their mestizo environments rather than political statements. Some of these arts are now held up as symbols of Sino-Indonesian integration. Drawing on Bakhtin's distinction between organic and intentional hybridity, he describes the shadow puppet form now generally known as *wayang kulit Cina-Jawa* as "the organic expression of a highly talented Yogyakarta bicultural artist," Gan Thwan Sing, not "a conscious negotiation of Chinese identity" (166). This form dramatizes Tang dynasty narratives but is performed in Javanese with gamelan accompaniment, and uses puppets with the same basic morphology as *wayang kulit*, bearing "little resemblance to anything known in China" and thus "testing the limits of terms such as 'Chinese'" (75). Over the last decade, this art has been revived and revised in performances, publications, and exhibitions that proclaim it as an example of the capacities of local Chinese to "'become Javanese' and, by extension, Indonesian" (73).

In contrast, the Chinese of West Kalimantan were of Hakka derivation and preferred a little-known form of string puppet theater from western Fujian known as *chiao theu* in Hakka or *wayang gantung* in Indonesian. This form has made few concessions to Indonesian modernity, and the one remaining troupe in Singkawang performs in Hakka to conservative, *totok* audiences at local rituals and occasionally for multicultural festivals.

A major strength of this study is the author's capacity to balance Chinese- and Indonesian-language sources—and to bring sinocentric and diasporic sources into productive dialogue. Chinese-language reports of opera troupes that departed from the mainland to tour Southeast Asia are linked to accounts of these itinerant companies' reception, allowing an assessment of the particular genres of opera to which audiences were exposed, starting with the Hokkien *gaojixaxi* troupe Fujinxing (Fortunate and Golden Prosperity), which undertook multiple tours of the region between 1833 and 1844 (27). A highpoint of the book is a detailed account of the playwright Wang Renshu, better known under his pen name Baren, who lived in exile in Sumatra between 1942 and 1946 and returned to Indonesia in 1949–51 as the first People's Republic of China (PRC) ambassador. Baren's Chinese-language play *Temple of the Five Ancestors* (1946), commissioned by the Medan-based theater group Xin Zhongguo Juyishe (New China Dramatic Society), revisits a nineteenth-century uprising in Deli as a means to generate "proletarian solidarity" and align "Indonesian interests with the People's Republic of China" (86). This rebellion is also the subject of a play by the same name written in Chinese thirteen years later by the Sumatran Chinese journalist Shalihong (also known as Li Jing and Sinshe Rusli). Stenberg mines the scripts of the plays, memoirs, and journalistic and academic accounts, and situates these plays in terms of trends in the writing of historical dramas in the PRC and a florescence of Chinese spoken drama in Indonesia in the 1940s and '50s. This chapter is, as far as I am aware, the first academic study of Chinese-language spoken theater in Indonesia, and it opens up a significant field for future inquiries.

Another of the book's strengths is the way Stenberg relates historical and contemporary materials, attending to the resiliency of traditions, lines of continuity and changes in performance practices, revivals, appropriations, and ruptures. Many arts, including *xiqu*, *potehi*, and *chiao theu*/*wayang gantung*, are able to weather the anti-Chinese policies of the New Order by changing their names, narrowing their scope of activity, and transforming into ritual arts performed in temples and linked closely to legitimated religious celebrations. Two active *gezaixi* operatic troupes in the South Sumatra capital of Palembang, South Sumatra Arts and Tridharma Arts, are part of a continuous history of Hokkien-language operatic performance, interrupted only briefly between 1965 and 1972 and again between 1980 and 1982. Before the New Order, Palembang's *gezaixi* companies were enriched by teachers imported from China, which was no longer possible after 1965. But even during the New Order they were able to import *gezaixi* recordings from Taiwan and Fujian, enabling Palembang performers to keep abreast of current practices and resist acculturation and hybridization. Since Reformasi, ties to the strong Hokkien communities of Medan and the professional *gezaiqi* companies of mainland China and Taiwan have tightened.

The celebration of Cap Go Meh (the Lantern Festival) in Singkawang stands in contrast. This is now a state-sponsored festival, both a defining moment for the display of local Chinese identity and also a "civic and multiethnic project" (159) touted as a highlight of the Indonesian touristic calendar. In addition to contending for the title of the "longest dragon in Asia" (158), a key part of this event is a procession of hundreds of Chinese and Dayak mediums (*tatung*) who are possessed by Chinese and Dayak spirits. Demonstrating the power of the possessing spirits, they parade "in a state of trance—gesticulate, balance, scream. Many have pierced their cheeks, ears, or lips with skewers; on the ends of some skewers, oranges are impaled" (155). This practice is interpreted alternately as the unique survival of a Hakka rite that disappeared from mainland China under Mao or as a synthesis of Chinese and Dayak culture. The public visibility and funding of this ecstatic enactment have made it a target over the last decade of Islamist agitators objecting to its foreignness and syncretism, and in 2011, Cap Go Meh celebrations (*tatung*) were banned by the mayor.

Stenberg describes this book as a reconciliation of two of his established academic interests—overseas Chinese communities and Chinese performance, especially *xiqu*. Having lived for years in mainland China, Hong Kong, and Taipei, he arrived with particular understandings of Chineseness that were challenged in the research he conducted starting with his first trip to Indonesia in 2011. The book is informed by a general appreciation of the significance of the arts in migrant and diasporic communities and the dynamics of identity formation. It is also strong in its delineations of institutional histories of artistic companies and cultural associations. Less space is devoted to analyzing specific performances or describing the generic constraints of performance forms. So in the section on Hakka string puppets, no information is provided on the size of figures, the materials used in making them, the number of strings, or the means of control—all critical data for students of puppetry.

The focus on Chineseness as expressed in performance means that Indonesian Chinese practitioners active in non-Chinese art forms receive short thrift. The Bandung-based musician Tan Deseng is profiled as a leading Sundanese musical artist who is trained in traditional forms such as Cianjuran and "adept at mixing Sundanese and Chinese music together" (129). Interviewed in 2013, Tan griped that he merited inclusion in a who's who of Indonesian Chinese but was not awarded with an entry in a standard Sundanese encyclopedia. But the Surabaya impresario Yap Gwan Thay and Yogyakarta-based dancer Didik Nini Thowok are mentioned in passing, and there are no references to the record producer Tan Hoe Lo or actor Tan Tjeng Bok.[3] The innovative Soei Ban Lian Malay-language theater company, which combined features of Chinese opera and Malay operetta and enjoyed huge popularity in the first decades of the twentieth century, is mentioned twice (32, 103), but with different spellings and without much context. To be fair, Stenberg is aware of this shortcoming and attributes his focus on Chinese forms to his "field of competence" (169), as much as his analytical concerns. There is clearly room for another book here.

Stenberg expresses subdued optimism for the future of Sino-Indonesian performance and other forms of public display in Indonesia. Museums of Chinese culture popping up around Indonesia (including the Chinese pavilion and associated Confucian temple in the Taman Mini Indonesia Indah theme park), revitalization of exchange relations between Chinese Indonesian cultural organizations with Chinese artists and associations abroad, revival of Chinese language use, large-scale musicals with Chinese themes playing in Jakarta's premiere theaters, pride taken in Chinese identity, new sources of patronage like the Yensen Project of Mojokerto (which supports *potehi*), the inclusion of Chinese arts in university curricular and extracurricular programming, and increased involvement of non-Chinese people in Chinese arts, including *potehi*, are hopeful signs. The shadow of the 2017 imprisonment of Ahok, the Chinese governor of Jakarta, and ongoing "fears that prominent displays of Chinese culture and identity might . . . eventually produce a backlash," dampen the "euphoria" around the reemergence of Chinese cultural expression (16). However, with Sino-Indonesian artists and cultural activists studying up on how diasporic communities outside of Indonesia (not only Chinese) are making strategic use of heritage arts to claim space in multicultural societies and contribute to civil society, there is still room for growth and development ahead.

---

[3] For recent biographies, see Fandy Hutari and Deddy Otara, *Tan Tjeng Bok: Seniman Tiga Zaman (1898–1985)* (Jakarta: KPG, 2019), and Madoka Fukuoka and Hitoshi Furuya, *Indonesian Cross-Gender Dancer Didik Nini Thowok* (n.p.: Ōsakadaigakushuppankai, 2018).

Lightning Source UK Ltd.
Milton Keynes UK
UKHW050735190122
397366UK00003B/11